Dogs

Recognising and Identifying

Dogs

Recognising and Identifying

Picture credits:
E. A. Baumbach / Okapia KG: pp. 96, 97; Rolf Bender / Okapia KG:
p. 25; Bernd Brinkmann / Okapia KG: pp. 14, 66, 68, 80, 112, 122, 125;
Zack Burris Inc. / Okapia KG: p. 126; Cheryl A. Ertelt / Okapia KG: p. 50;
Hermeline / Cogis / Okapia KG: p. 41; Barbara von Hoffmann /
Okapia KG: pp. 112, 115; J-L Klein & M-L Hubert / Okapia KG: pp. 16,
56, 57, 64, 73, 84, 92, 93, 127; Labat / Cogis / Okapia KG: pp. 49, 104;
Lanceau / Cogis / Okapia KG: pp. 54, 113, 125; Hans Reinhard / Okapia
KG: p. 73; Christine Steimer / Okapia KG: pp. 7, 64; Klaus Sudbrack /
Okapia KG: p. 23; Karl Gottfried Vock / Okapia KG: p. 21
All remaining illustrations are from the archives of the publisher.

Table of Contents

The Most Important Breeds

Approximately 340 dog breeds are officially recognised worldwide. In the brief portraits that follow we have tried to introduce a wide range of breeds, naturally including all the best known dogs, but also those that are less familiar and have distinctive characteristics.

As there are breeds that share many traits in common, it is logical to combine some of them into groups, such as the terriers or windhounds.

Regarding the descriptions of various dogs, the sizes and weights given can only be approximate. It is impossible to know precisely how large animals will become when fully grown.

The height given refers to the dog's shoulder, rather than the head. Male dogs are often substantially, even visibly, larger than females of the same breed.

As you read this information, keep in mind that a purebred dog from a reputable breeder will be in accordance with the standards of the breed.

Nevertheless, any individual dog may not incorporate all the qualities of its breed as distinctly as described in the ideal of the breed.

For example, how well a dog interacts with children depends less on its breed than on the dog's being trained to interact with them from a young age.

A dog's experience also plays an essential role. Dogs that have been teased by children can develop a basic dislike or mistrust of children.

Fortunately, not only negative qualities, but also positive ones interact with the personality of the dog at hand. Each dog is an individual with its own special qualities which make it unmistakable and loveable, and that is the beauty of it all.

Hunting Dogs

Barbet

Size and build

The Barbet is a French gundog that was used to fetch fowl out of the water. It looks like a farm dog. Weighing between 20 and 30 kg (44–66 lb) at a height of at least 25 up to 55 cm (10–22 in), it is strong and stocky. The back is somewhat curved and the tail begins rather low on the body, curving upward at an angle.

Coat

A Barbet's coat is woolly, curly and long, providing good protection from inclement weather, and may become matted if the dog is not groomed properly. There is a wide variety of colouration including black, grey, chestnut, yellow, ivory or brown and white.

Character and disposition

Although Barbets are hunters, they are adaptable and have many agreeable qualities. They are considered happy, intelligent, devoted and obedient dogs—and great swimmers.

Living conditions

If you are looking for a companionable family dog, the Barbet is an excellent choice. It gets along extremely well with children, and needs a lot of exercise to feel its best.

Bavarian Mountain Hound

Size and build

This medium-size hound reaches a shoulder height of up to 50 cm (20 in).

Coat

The coat of a Bavarian Mountain Hound is thick, smooth and tends to be matt rather than shiny. They are found in several different shades of red and gold, which are sometimes interspersed with light-coloured hair as well.

Character and disposition

This medium-size dog was bred for its excellent tracking skills and persistence, and is distinguished by its reliability, intelligence and liveliness.

Living conditions

Exercise is just what this dog needs. If the dog is to be used as a hunting dog you will have to train it carefully and continue with regular training sessions.

Billy

Size and build

The Billy is a tall and powerful dog with a graceful appearance. It grows to 60 to 70 cm (24–28 in) tall and weighs about 25 to 30 kg (55–66 lb). It has a strong back with a slightly rounded rump.

Coat

Coarse, short hair is typical for the Billy. This dog may be white or light brown as well as white with markings in shades of orange or lemon yellow. Black spots in the hair are considered undesirable.

Character and disposition

This hunting dog is exceptionally fast and only rarely tires out. It displays extraordinary stamina and energy when hunting.

Living conditions

The Billy gets along well with other dogs and with children. Nonetheless, because of its still strong hunting instincts, it is not suitable as a family dog.

Chesapeake Bay Retriever

Size and build

This gorgeous hunting dog can reach a height of up to 70 cm (28 in), and with a weight of 30 kg (66 lb) is not especially heavy. Its build is solid and well-proportioned with sturdy limbs. The head is fairly wide with a slightly rounded skull. The Chesapeake Bay Retriever has an unusual characteristic that is typical of many water dogs: it has webbed toes.

Coat

Hidden underneath the dog's dense, short top coat is an oily, waterproof undercoat. The top layer of hair may be slightly wavy on the back.

The Chesapeake Bay Retriever is found in all shades of brown and some yellow tones. White markings on the toes and chest are not considered flaws.

Character and disposition

This breed combines a host of very agreeable character traits. It tends to be intelligent, quick to learn, courageous and devoted; however its hunting instinct remains strong.

Living conditions

This powerful dog needs a lot of space and a lot of exercise. Bred to fetch fowl from cold water, it is well suited to exercising in the water. It does not get along with other dogs in every situation, but usually does quite well with children. Since this retriever is active and learns readily, you should be prepared to undertake some kind of purposeful activity with it.

Cocker Spaniel

Size and build

These popular dogs have a compact and strong back which slopes slightly toward the tail, combined with a robust musculature. The English Cocker Spaniel, which is slightly larger than the American Cocker Spaniel, stands about 40 cm (16 in) tall and weighs between 12 and 14 kg (27–32 lb). The English Cocker Spaniel has a rounder head and a somewhat more elongated muzzle than its American cousin.

Coat

The English Cocker Spaniel has flat, silky hair which may be slightly wavy. The legs are feathered. The hair on the head is shorter and especially fine. An American Cocker Spaniel has much longer hair. Both versions

come in many different colours, whether solid or in combination.

Character and disposition

Cocker Spaniels are far from calm dogs. They are clever, intelligent and lively in a pleasant way, and can develop very close relationships with their owners.

Living conditions

To train this veritable bundle of energy, which is quite willing to learn, requires a patient, strict hand that is at the same time very loving. A well-trained Cocker Spaniel is a delightful pet that gets along extremely well with other dogs and children. You do not have to provide a house with a garden for a Cocker Spaniel, but it will need a lot of exercise, nonetheless.

German Wirehaired Pointer

Size and build

Dogs of this hunting breed commonly stand between 55 and 70 cm (22–28 in) tall. They may weigh up to 30 kg (66 lb). They have a relatively short and straight back with a long, slightly sloped rump. The head is short and they have a well-developed muzzle.

Coat

The coat is wiry and coarse and lies quite close to the dog's skin. Inconspicuous colours such as medium-brown or brown with white are the norm.

Character and disposition

If this gundog has been properly trained to hunt, its quarry will only rarely escape. The German Wirehaired Pointer excels at many hunting tasks, in particular retrieving. It is also very loyal and watchful.

Living conditions

You should only keep a German Wirehaired Pointer as a pet if you

live in a house with a garden. This dog usually has no problems with children and other dogs.

German Longhaired Pointer

Size and build

Individual dogs of this old hunting breed can grow to be taller than 60 cm (24 in). Their weight is usually between 25 and 30 kg (55–66 lb). These dogs have a noble, elongated head and their physique has a lot of similarities with the German Wirehaired Pointer.

Coat

The hair is from 3 to 5 cm (1–2 in) long, and may be even longer on the chest and belly. Several colours and shades may occur, for example, solid brown in a range of shades or all one colour with white markings.

Character and disposition

The German Longhaired Pointer is an obedient and—with proper training—an extremely reliable hunting dog. It is a good-nature creature, but can develop the necessary aggressiveness when called for.

Living conditions

German Longhaired Pointers generally have no problems with children and with other dogs; on the contrary, they develop wonderful patience toward children.

This pleasant demeanour makes them good family pets. Since they were bred as hunting dogs, however, they will need to run even if they are kept as companion dogs.

English Setter

Size and build

Dogs of this breed look strong and well-proportioned, yet still light on their feet. Fully grown English Setters stand about 60 cm (24 in) tall and weigh between 25 and 30 kg (55–66 lb). They have an elongated head with a long muzzle. The long, straight tail sports a feathering of soft, long hair.

Coat

The coat of an English Setter is soft, silky and of medium length. The hair on the head is clearly shorter than elsewhere on its body. The coat is usually mottled in any of several colour combinations, usually including white.

Character and disposition

English Setters are distinguished by a wide range of positive qualities that include loyalty, devotion, and a genuine passion for exercise.

Living conditions

This hunting dog can be readily trained to excel at various types of hunting, whether it be in the water or in the field. If you intend to keep this dog as a pet you will have to provide it with opportunities to roam freely in open spaces, as it needs a great deal of exercise to remain healthy. If a dog of this breed is trained with a loving hand, you will find it an easy, agreeable friend and companion who gets on very well with other dogs and children.

Field Spaniel

Size and build

When fully grown, this hunting spaniel will attain a height of about 45 cm (18 in) and should weigh between 15 and 25 kg (33–55 lb).

Coat

The coat of a Field Spaniel should not be too short. It may be smooth or slightly wavy, but in either case the hair must be thick and glossy. Frequently found colours include mahogany and black.

Character and disposition

Dogs of this breed have a sweet disposition. They are sensitive, lively and adventurous. They are enthusiastic about hunting.

Living conditions

The Field Spaniel is a gundog, bred to retrieve birds. It can be kept as a pet, although it is advisable to provide it with a house and a garden rather than a flat with no direct access to the outdoors. Having the chance to run is a key factor for the well-being of this agile dog. Otherwise they are easy to deal with, enjoying the company of children and their own kind.

Flat-coated Retriever

Size and build

This well-proportioned dog may reach a height of 60 cm (24 in) and weighs about 30 kg (66 lb). It has a long neck that flows into the muscular back and straight, short croup. The limbs are strong. The head is rather long with a powerful, long muzzle.

Coat

The glossy coat of the Flat-coated Retriever lies close to its body. It is thick, fine and long with a thick undercoat.

Character and disposition

The Flat-coated Retriever has many lovely characteristics: it is an intelligent and eager learner, easy to raise and train. It is also a lively and responsive dog with a gentle, people-loving nature. It can develop great devotion

Living conditions

These hunting dogs are especially suited for retrieving fowl. You can keep the Flat-coated Retriever as a pet, as well, but you will need to have a lot of room and take the dog on long walks. These animals have a strong drive to run which will need to be satisfied. These well-balanced creatures get on

very well with children and other dogs.

Golden Retriever

Size and build

This magnificent dog can get as tall as 60 cm (24 in) and weighs about 30 kg (66 lb). It has a well proportioned, rectangular build. It has a wide skull with a well developed muzzle and a distinct stop. The paws are round.

Coat

Golden is the key word here. The coat of a Golden Retriever may be anywhere from golden light brown to golden yellow, as well

as cream coloured or wheat yellow. Markings are not considered desirable, though a very few white hairs may be part of the coat. The hair is of medium length and can be slightly wavy or straight. The top coat lies closely over a thick undercoat. Longer hair can be found as feathering on the tail, under the belly and on the chest, as well as on the back of the front legs.

Character and disposition

The Golden Retriever is a gentle and patient friend and companion. They are relatively easy to train and can be especially de-

voted to their people. This is an ardent gundog that loves to retrieve game during the hunt.

Living conditions

The Golden Retriever belongs to the breeds that can be used in several different ways. From the ranks of hunters you may hear occasional complaints about how trendy this breed has become and that it no longer has its original qualities. You may hear similar complaints about other breeds, as well, and they may be well founded. A dog is not a decorative object. In fact, when choosing a dog you should always consider whether you can keep it in accordance with its natural tendencies. The Golden Retriever thrives when it is busy and well exercised. A house on a large property is a suitable place for it. This dog gets on extremely well with children. As a working dog the Golden Retriever may provide valuable services, for example, as a rescue dog.

Gordon Setter

Size and build

There is a resemblance between this breed and the English Setter that can hardly be overlooked. Overall the Gordon Setter looks

17

somewhat stronger, though they don't differ much in size and weight. The Gordon Setter will get as tall as 65 cm (26 in) and weighs about 30 kg (66 lb).

Coat

Silky, long hair is characteristic for these dogs. The hair is straight or somewhat wavy, and it is longer around the ears, chest and tail. The coat is a deep, glossy black with distinctive mahogany markings. The markings can be seen on the muzzle, above the eyes and on the dog's legs.

Grooming

To keep a Gordon Setter looking respectable, you will have to invest some time to comb and brush it thoroughly and often.

Character and disposition

This dignified gundog has a range of agreeable qualities. It is loving, adaptable and devoted, but not over submissive.

Living conditions

When trained appropriately, this dog can be used in various ways during hunting, especially for re-

trieving game after the shots have been fired. If you keep a Gordon Setter as a pet, you should give it ample occasion to run. As with many large dogs that love to run, a house with a garden is prerequisite for this dog's well-being. Because of its patience, it gets on very well with children

Griffon Fauve de Bretagne

Size and build

This powerful French dog stands up to 55 cm (22 in) and weighs 25 kg (55 lb). It has a slightly rectangular shape and a pointed tail of medium length. Its ears hang down.

Coat

Dogs of this breed have a distinctive, very hard and coarse coat of medium length with softer hair around their ears. They are found in various shades of brownish red, light red or wheat yellow. Bright shades are especially admired.

Character and disposition

The Griffon Fauve de Bretagne is a passionate hunter, very lively and full of energy. In addition, this dog has a friendly disposition and is very devoted to its owner.

Living conditions

A dog of this kind, originally bred centuries ago to hunt wolves, still does best in the hands of a hunter. In this situation it can get the exercise it needs in accordance with its natural drive and can make use of its outstanding sense of smell.

A flat is not an appropriate home for this dog. It gets on very well with other dogs.

Hanoverian Hound

Size and build

This powerful, massive hunting dog may reach a height of 60 cm (24 in) and weighs well over 30 kg (66 lb). Its head is medium-sized and it has a long, strong

19

throat clad with loose skin. It has a deep chest and the rump slopes down at an angle. The front legs are thicker than its hind legs. This dog has relatively short legs with strong, round paws.

Coat

The glossy, smooth coat of this breed is comparatively short and soft. The coat can have different shades of colour with markings—among them are grey-brown, red-brown, golden-red and deep gold. The coat may also be brindled.

Grooming

Taking care of this rather short coat doesn't require much effort.

Character and disposition

This hunting dog is intelligent and can be trained more easily than others. It can also show great devotion and loyalty. It develops great stamina while hunting.

Living conditions

A lot of exercise and a task are what you need to provide for a Hanoverian Hound. In light of this, this dog will thrive when owned by a hunter. Because it is also an adaptable creature, it feels comfortable as part of a family, as well.

Harrier

Size and build

The resemblance between this hunting dog and the Beagle cannot be denied. The Harrier is larger, however: generally up to 55 cm (22 in). The body appears rather stocky overall, in part because of the dog's relatively short legs and deep chest with a well-rounded rib cage. The head is medium in size and the neck is quite long.

Coat

The Harrier has comparatively short, coarse hair that lies close to the body. The typical coat is white

with large patches of colour, generally ranging through tan, black and brown.

Character and disposition

The long-established Harrier is an enthusiastic hunter. That activity gives it an opportunity to put its strong will and boundless stamina to good use.

This is an intelligent dog that learns quickly.

Living conditions

This dog is quite content in a pack of hunting dogs because it gets on very well with its own kind. It is used especially for hunting in flat terrain.

Irish Setter

Size and build

This elegant hunting dog usually stands a bit over 60 cm (24 in) tall and weighs about 20 to 25 kg

(44–55 lb). Compared with other setters, the Irish Setter's physique looks more slender and agile. This difference is also visible in its somewhat narrow chest.

Coat

The coat of an Irish Setter is long, silky and smooth with long, feathering hair on the back of the legs, on the tail, as well as on the throat and chest. The colour of this very elegant animal's coat is mahogany.

Character and disposition

This gundog, bred to retrieve game, has a lot of energy and is even said to be a bit wild on occasion.

Nevertheless, it is intelligent and can be trained. With patient training this setter can be turned into a hunting dog with very useful qualities. In addition to its enthusiasm and decisive disposition, this dog is also very devoted and loyal.

Living conditions

The Irish Setter was bred to be used both in the field and in the water during hunting. If you intend to keep this dog as a pet you must commit yourself to providing it with a lot of exercise. To do otherwise would not be in accordance with the dog's nature.

As rule, this agile dog gets on very well with children. Irish Setters have a reputation for occasionally acting in a rather moody and even unpredictable manner toward other dogs and strangers.

Labrador Retriever

Size and build

A fully-grown Labrador Retriever can be 60 cm (24 in) or taller and weighs between 30 and 35 kg (66–77 lb). On the whole, this dog is powerful, muscular and well-proportioned.

The head is rectangular in shape, relatively wide with a long, strong muzzle. Its neck and chest are also powerful.

The Labrador Retriever has sturdy limbs and compact, round paws.

Coat

The coat of this breed is dense, flat, short, and somewhat hard—such a coat protects this swimming dog's body from the water. A Labrador Retriever usually has a coat of one solid colour. Black, shades of brown and yellow are quite common.

Character and disposition

Working and living with this dog is a genuine pleasure for the human being involved. Labrador Retrievers are extremely intelligent and quick to react, hardworking and obedient.

Once bred to work in the water, some are still trained as gundogs. Today, however, others serve as guide dogs or trackers.

Labrador Retrievers distinguish themselves with their exceptional devotion for their owners.

Living conditions

If you intend to keep this working dog as a companion you will have to provide it with ample opportunity for activity and exercise. The Labrador is neither a lap dog nor a bore, and needs to have something to do. In general, it enjoys the company of children and gets on well with other dogs.

Muensterlaender Pointer

Size and build

There are two types of Muensterlaenders, large (up to 60 cm/ 24 in tall) and small (about 56 cm/22 in). Both are characterised by their elegant physique, and they look very much alike. Typical for both is a strong, muscular neck of medium length, powerful croup and robust limbs.

Coat

The beautiful coat of the Large Muensterlaender is a distinctive white with black patches and/or spots. It can also have black roan or ticking. The Small Muensterlaender is white with liver spots or patches or both; there is a brown roan version as well. With both breeds the coat is of medium length and firm.

Character and disposition

Muensterlaenders are attentive, obedient and watchful dogs. They distinguish themselves with their intelligence and ability to learn. They can be passionate hunting dogs.

Living conditions

As the name indicates, the Muensterlaender Pointer is used as a

pointer when hunting. They can take on other hunting tasks as well, such as flushing and retrieving. If you keep the Small or Large Muensterlaender purely as a pet you will have to make sure that the dog gets a lot of exercise and activity. A house with a garden is a good starting point. With regard to exercise you do not always have to take the dog for a walk. As with many a dog that loves to run, the Muenster-laender can be taken along when hiking or it can run along for a good stretch next to a bicycle.

English Pointer

Size and build

A Pointer can grow up to 60 cm (24 in) tall and weigh from 20 to 25 kg (44–55 lb). Its body has a slightly elongated rectangular form. These animals have a dynamic and powerful look. Their

front legs, like their muscular hind quarters, are strong. The head is broad and flat with a strong and pronounced muzzle.

Coat

The coat of the Pointer is short and glossy. Lemon, orange and black are occasionally found as solids. More often, however, they appear in combination, always on a white base coat.

Character and disposition

The Pointer is an energetic, enthusiastic hunter with an exceptional sense of smell and great stamina. It has an intelligent manner and is eager to learn.

Living conditions

The Pointer is not a dog for the city. Still, it is not completely un- suitable as a family pet since it is generally friendly with children. With sensitive guidance it may even become affectionate. However, lots of exercise is essential for this animal. This dog would certainly be living more fully according to its nature as a hunting dog.

Poodle Pointer

Size and build

This German hunting dog is well known to the cognoscenti. It can grow somewhere between 60 and 70 cm (24–28 in) tall and weighs between 25 and 30 kg (55–66 lb). The Poodle Pointer looks powerful but not heavy. The length of the head and muzzle are well-balanced in relation to one another. The limbs are strong and the paws are round.

Coat

The Poodle Pointer has a firm to hard coat of medium length on top of a dense undercoat. Different shades of brown are typical.

Character and disposition

This dog is active and a hard worker. It is straight forward and relatively easy to train.

Living conditions

A hunting dog like this does not belong in the city. It will thrive in the hands of a hunter, where it can put its skills to use in various ways. If you keep this dog as a pet you should provide it with a lot of space, if possible a large property. Its relationship to other dogs as well as to children is unproblematic.

Weimaraner

Size and build

This big, impressive dog can be as large as 70 cm (28 in), and its weight will vary according to its height, up to 30 kg (66 lb). The head of the Weimaraner is of medium size.

The jaw is strong and but not pointed. The Weimaraner has a very strong back and comparatively long limbs.

Coat

The shorthair is the more traditional type of Weimaraner, but there is also a longhaired variety that sports a top coat with hair of about 3 cm (1 in) basic length and even longer hair in some areas, for example the chest. Typical coat colours for Weimaraners are primarily grey of metallic sheen, sometimes with other shades blended in, such as roe grey or mouse grey.

Character and disposition

The Weimaraner is characterised by its industriousness and great stamina, and it may easily develop some aggressive traits while working. The breed is also known for its calm manner as well as its obedience.

Living conditions

The Weimaraner is used as a pointer during hunting. If you keep it as a pet you will have to make sure that this animal has plenty of exercise and lots of opportunities to walk. Keeping this type of dog in a smaller flat is not a good idea. This dog is not known for any problematic behaviour with either children or its own species.

Hounds

Afghan Hound (Tazi, Afghan)

Size and build

The typical Afghan look is tall and elegant. When fully grown it will reach a height of 61 to 74 cm (24–29 in) and weigh up to 28 kg (62 lb). Its medium-length body has a straight and muscular back.

Coat

A fine, long and silky coat distinguishes this lightning-quick sprinter. The hair on the face and back is substantially shorter than elsewhere on its body. Afghans sometimes have a black mask on their face, quite apart from the colouring of the rest of their body. Tan and golden are the most popular colours for the Afghan Hound.

Character and disposition

An Afghan Hound is proud, courageous and extremely sensitive, and does best when lavished with attention. It needs real affection and does not readily trust strangers. If abused, this dog will remember it for a very long time.

Suitable surroundings

There are three preconditions that make the Afghan a dog that is not just for anyone: it requires a lot of care and attention, a tremendous amount of exercise and generous amounts of food. In other ways, however, Afghans are uncomplicated dogs. They can get on well with children and to some extent with other dogs, as well.

Borzoi (Russian Wolfhound)

Size and build

The Borzoi is a large wolfhound. It may reach a height of up to 82 cm (32 in) and weighs between 35 and 45 kg (77–99 lb).

A Borzoi has a distinctive long, narrow head with a tapered muzzle. Its stomach is tucked up. Its back feet resemble the paws of a hare. The European Borzoi tends to be slightly taller than its Russian cousin.

Coat

Most common are Borzois that are pure white or white with coloured patches (brown, grey, yellow, red). Their hair is long and often curly, but it may also be wavy or straight.

Character and disposition

The Borzoi may be understood as a proud and reserved animal. It may be somewhat distant and at times even unfriendly toward strangers, but is devoted and obedient toward the people it knows and loves.

Living conditions

A lot of space and a great deal of exercise are absolutely essential for the well-being of this Russian courser. Though a Borzoi will not always get along with other dogs, it will usually accept others of the same species if they belong to the same household. Its relationship toward children is unproblematic.

Basenji

Size and build

This small hunting hound is a very old breed and will grow up to

48 cm (19 in) tall and reach a weight of about 11 kg (24 lb). It has a comparatively short and straight back. Its tail is set high on the body and curls upward over the back once or twice. When a Basenji perks up its ears, the forehead creases.

Coat

A typical colouration is fox-brown with white markings, but Basenjis may also be black and white with patches of red. Yellow and cream colouring is not considered desirable. The coat is thick and short, but very fine and silky.

Character and disposition

Basenjis are known to be well-balanced, patient and devoted.

Living conditions

Basenjis can be kept in a city, but they are dogs who love to run and require a great deal of exercise. They are suitable as pets for families with children.

Basset Hound

Size and build

When we talk about bassets, we generally have a Basset Hound in mind. A Basset Hound is one of the heaviest representatives of the basset famil. With short legs and a rather long, low profile overall a Basset Hound may stand up to 38 cm (15 in) tall.

The various parts of its body are short and thick with large, heavy

Living conditions

The Basset Hound was bred to be a small game hunter. As long as it has sufficient opportunity to exercise, it makes a lovely family dog and can even live in less than spacious quarters. Its relationship with children and other dogs is usually unproblematic.

Beagle

Size and build

The Beagle is one of the smaller hounds, growing to be no more than 40 cm (16 in) tall and weighing about 15 kg (33 lb). There is also an even smaller type of Beagle called a "Pocket Beagle", which is just 25 cm (10 in) high. These miniature dogs enjoyed great popularity in the early 20th century.

Coat

A thick, relatively short coat is characteristic for Beagles. They come in all the typical hound colours—white, brown, black and yellow—or some combination thereof.

Character and disposition

Beagles are clever, exuberant and courageous. In addition to a generally sweet nature, it might show a little stubbornness.

paws to match. The American Basset Hound is a bit more compact and not as massive as the English variant.

Coat

The coat of the Basset Hound is smooth, straight and glossy, and the hair should be neither too coarse nor too fine. Many different colours are acceptable.

Character and disposition

The Basset Hound is known to be of a peaceful and gentle nature, but it may show a stubborn streak.

Living conditions

Beagles are great hunting dogs. If you want to keep one in an urban setting you have to provide some kind of substitution for traditional hunting grounds. Long walks in the woods make this dog happy. Beagles get on very well with children and other dogs.

Bloodhound (Saint Hubert Hound)

Size and build

Bloodhounds are powerfully built dogs. They can reach a height of 60 cm (24 in) or more, and move their massive bodies—they weigh around 40 to 48 kg (88–105 lb)—

with a regal gait. The head is large, long and slim. The ears are set low and hang down softly.

Coat

This strong chap has short fine hair which is coarse on most of its body, except for the head and ears, where it is silky soft. More than one kind of colouration is allowed for Bloodhounds: the hair may be black, tan or red. Especially noticeable are the typical folds or wrinkles on the cheeks and forehead.

Character and disposition

Possibly because of its name, the Bloodhound has not always en-

joyed a positive reputation with some people. This is entirely unfair. The name does not point to this dog's thirst for blood, but rather to the purity of its bloodline. When treated well— which is a prerequisite for good behaviour in all dogs—the Bloodhound develops a high level of obedience, devotion and a gentle nature. If treated badly, it will

react rather disagreeably, and may tend to act aggressively and to bite people.

Living conditions

Bloodhounds need a lot of space, and are certainly happiest in a home with a garden in which to run. If you don't have the required space you should recon-

sider whether the Bloodhound is a suitable dog for your family. One strong quality is that they get along well with children. They can readily be trained as scent dogs, and if used to track they need regular training to stay in top form. A Bloodhound requires a consistent and fair leader in any case.

Braque Français (French Pointer)

Size and build

There are two types of this old line of French gundogs: the Braque Francais de Grande Taille stands just under 70 cm (28 in) and weighs about 30 kg (66 lb), while the smaller Braque Francais de Petite Taille may reach 60 cm (24 in) and weighs about 20 kg (44 lb).

French Pointers are strong dogs with a straight back and comparatively long, muscular limbs.

Coat

The French Pointer has thick, short hair all over its body. The hair is fine, especially on its head. It comes in various colours, often brown brindle or white and brown speckled. Black spots are not desired in this breed.

Character and disposition

The French Pointer has a gentle and well-meaning disposition. At the same time, it is a sporting dog and thus very lively. This breed readily responds to obedience training, a tendency that is an asset if the dog is being trained as a hunting companion. The French Pointer also has tremendous stamina.

Living conditions

Because of their typical traits, these dogs adapt well which is an advantage on the domestic front.

With their need to move, it is best if they can exercise in a garden in addition to regular walks. They usually have no problems with other dogs and are friendly toward children, as well.

Dachshund (Teckel)

Size and build

Popularly known as the Dachshund, Teckels are a well-known short-legged dog breed that includes many different varieties. The various Dachshunds differ in their size and in the quality of their hair.

Coat

When distinguishing the breeds by size, one takes into consideration not only shoulder and wither height, but the chest size as well. There are Standard, Miniature and Toy Dachshunds, and these are further grouped by hair type, so that there are Smooth, Wirehaired and Longhaired Dachshunds of each size.

Character and disposition

Although these dogs have become popular companion dogs because of their pleasant character, Dachshunds were originally bred for hunting. Dachshund

literally means "badger dog" in German, and that is what they were bred to hunt. The short legs that may look comical to us are actually an asset for these

through crossbreeding. One of the Wirehaired Dachshund's ancestors, for example, is the Dandie Dinmont Terrier, and among the ancestors of the Longhaired

earthdogs, specially bred for their ability to "go to ground", or follow game into its burrow and either flush it out or hold it still for the hunter to dig out. Their low, long form and strong musculature are ideal for digging into burrows.

Types

The Smooth Dachshund is the oldest type; the other varieties have been developed over time

Dachshund are a number of other game-flushing breeds.

Dalmatian

Size and build

These long-legged dogs reach a height of 50 to 60 cm (20–24 in) and weigh about 20 to 25 kg (44–55 lb).

A Dalmation typically has a well-proportioned, muscular and ele-

35

gant body. The head is of medium length with a long muzzle.

Coat

The hair of a Dalmatian is short, hard and grows densely. Even though the hairs are fine, they are not very soft. The ground colour of these dogs is pure white, with characteristic dark spots of various sizes spread all over the dog's coat. Puppies are born white and their unique pattern of spots slowly develops until the dog is approximately a year and a half old.

Character and disposition

Dalmatians are clever and very lively. They have a joyful nature and are easily trained—at least as long as they are treated lovingly.

Living conditions

The Dalmatian is well-suited as a family dog. It may show preference for one family member, but will love the others as well. Dalmatians are especially careful and sweet around children.

You can keep one in a city flat if you can give it substantial opportunities to run off its seemingly boundless energy.

Scottish Deerhound

Size and build

This comparatively rare dog can get up to 80 cm (32 in) and weighs about 50 kg (110 lb).

The Deerhound is a sturdy animal, but still has an elegant look to it. Its bones are heavier than those of any other windhound.

Coat

The coarse, dry hair is about 8 to 10 cm (3–4 in) long and comes in a range of colours such as slate grey, yellow or red-grey.

Character and disposition

This large hound is gentle and patient. It may develop great devotion toward its owner, and it is esteemed for its intelligence.

Living conditions

A large dog of this kind needs lots of exercise and is more easily kept in a house with a garden than a flat. The Deerhound can develop a good relationship with other dogs as well as children. It is also a competent watchdog.

German Hound (Deutsche Bracke)

Size and build

A fully grown German Hound will reach a height of about 50 cm (20 in) and weighs about 15 kg (33 lb). This dog has an elongated head, a well developed muzzle and is powerfully built.

Coat

The German Hound has thick, short and hard hair. The coat is red to tan with a dark saddle and white markings.

Character and disposition

This dog is a passionate hunter and possesses all the right qualities for the task. It generally gets along well with children and other dogs.

Living conditions

The German Hound needs to go hunting; this is one of those breeds that does not adapt well to life in an urban environment. This dog thrives especially when it lives with hunters.

Spanish Greyhound

Size and build

This large, slender windhound can get up to 70 cm (28 in) tall. It weighs approximately 25 kg (55 lb). Its physique looks both light and powerful at the same time.

It has a long, pointed muzzle. The front legs are straight, while the hind legs have clearly angulated hocks. There is a strong resemblance between the Spanish Greyhound and its English relative.

Coat

The coat of the Spanish Greyhound may have different colours

including black, red or the shade of a lion. The hair on these dogs is short, fine and thick.

Character and disposition

The Spanish Greyhound is often quite passionate, especially when it comes to racing.

On the other hand, it is also known to be obedient and occasionally reserved. This is an enthusiastic hunter.

Living conditions

This Spanish windhound generally gets on rather well with children. There are differing opinions on its relationship toward other dogs, and it may be quite aggressive during a race. Traditionally, the Spanish Greyhound is used for racing.

Greyhound (English Greyhound)

Size and build

The unmistakeable Greyhound will stand about 70 to 76 cm (28–30 in) when fully grown, but is rather light at just 30 to 35 kg (66–77 lb).

Their slender yet powerful rectangular body has the tucked up abdomen typical of the windhound group. The head is ex-

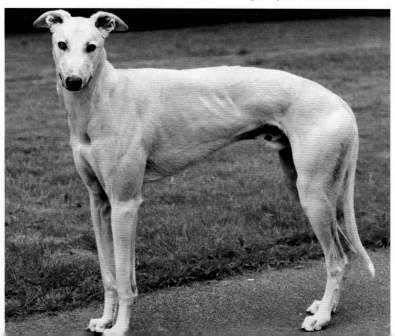

tremely long with a well-developed and pointed muzzle.

Coat

The English Greyhound has short, fine hair which is dense and glossy. The coat may be virtually any shade or combination of colours, either solid or with white markings.

Character and disposition

Bred to run, a Greyhound gives its all when it is racing, attaining maximum speeds up to 70 km/h (44 mph). At home, by contrast, it is rather shy, gentle and sensitive. This dog needs a lot of affection. Its positive qualities are rounded off by its watchfulness.

Living conditions

If you want to keep an English Greyhound in a flat you will have to provide it with daily opportunities to run and be physically active. In fact, some people do not recommend keeping a Greyhound as a companion dog under any circumstances. They require an immense amount of exercise and space to thrive. This elegant breed does insist on being left in peace when it is so moved, with the result that they do not always get along with children.

Irish Wolfhound

Size and build

If you have ever seen an Irish Wolfhound the image has probably stayed with you for a long while, because this animal is an impressive giant.

The tallest dogs in the world, some individuals of this breed stand far more than 80 cm (32 in) high, and a fully grown male averages an impressive 60 kg (130 lb) or even more.

This dog has a long and somewhat narrow head. Overall, its body appears very powerful without being massive. The paws are not particularly large and have a rounded shape with strong nails.

Coat

The coat of this awesome giant is hard and rough. It grows especially long above the eyes and under the chin, giving its face a bushy look.

Typical colourations include grey, red, fawn, white and black, among others.

Character and disposition

The Irish Wolfhound retains many characteristics from its original uses: hunting wolves and elk, and on battlefields. It has a gentle and calm disposition and is not easily disconcerted by anything. Nevertheless, it is by no means inattentive, but on the contrary, quite vigilant. In addition to that it displays great courage.

Living conditions

There is no doubt that a flat is not the appropriate place for a dog of this size. It is extremely important for the Irish Wolfhound to be able to move freely and get appropriate exercise.

As a rule, they get on well with children and make wonderful family pets. They are occasionally said to have a preference for forming a strong relationship with a single individual.

Lundehund (Puffin Dog)

Size and build

A fully grown Lundehund is between 30 and 36 cm (12–14 in) tall and weighs just 6 to 7 kg (13–16 lb). Its face has a fox-like expression. Bred specifically to hunt puffins, it has extra toes and extremely flexible joints.

Coat

This dog has a dense, coarse, close-lying coat. The undercoat is dense and soft. The coat may be of several different shades or colour combinations. Typical are white, grey, brown and black.

Character and disposition

The Lundehund is energetic, attentive and sociable and is naturally inclined to hunt.

Living conditions

If your dog will not be a hunter but a pet, it will need space and exercise. A house with a garden is appropriate. If that isn't possible you will have to plan on extensive walks. Other dogs and children are no problem for the Lundehund.

Hungarian Greyhound

Size and build

This Hungarian windhound has a shoulder height of 60 to 70 cm (24–28 in) and displays definite similarities to the English Greyhound. It weighs between 20 and just over 30 kg (44–66 lb).

Coat

The Hungarian Greyhound's coat is short and flat. There are many different colours and combinations such as black, tan and mocha, often in combination with black markings.

Character and disposition

This elegant windhound has a friendly nature. It makes an attentive and lively companion.

Living conditions

It goes without saying that these dogs need a lot of exercise. Regular training and a large property are preconditions for a Hungarian Greyhound to have a contented life. They are known to be friendly

toward children and are said to have no problems relating to other dogs, either.

Pharaoh Hound

Size and build

Pharaoh Hounds, a 3,000-year-old breed of hunting dog, grow to 65 to 70 cm (25–28 in) in height and weighs up to 20 kg (44 lb). They have an almost square form and a slender figure. The head is comparatively flat, and the muzzle tapers toward the nose. This dog has long legs.

Coat

This dog has a short, smooth and glossy coat. Typical colour combinations are various shades of tan through chestnut red, either solid or with a white mark, called a star, on the chest.

Character and disposition

Dogs of this breed range from independent to stubborn, yet are very companionable. Bred to hunt in ancient Egypt, they are passionate hunters and runners.

Living conditions

If you don't intend to work a Pharaoh Hound as a hunting dog, you will have to come up with a substitute activity that provides a lot of exercise and a focus for its many abilities. Provided these conditions are met, a Pharaoh Hound will be comfortable even in a small home. This dog has no problems with children or its own kind.

Italian Greyhound

Size and build

This southern breed of windhound can be up to 38 cm (15 in) tall. These exceptionally graceful animals are featherweights, generally weighing just 5 kg (11 lb). Overall, the Italian Greyhound looks like a miniature version of the Greyhound.

Among the characteristic features typical of these dogs are the narrow, pointed muzzle, its long, slender limbs and the tucked up stomach.

Coat

The coat of this small, fast dog is fine, short and lies close to the skin. Its colouration ranges through shades of grey, black, beige and white.

Character and disposition

The Italian Greyhound has a friendly, sensitive and lively disposition. These animals can be trained very easily and are highly adaptible to a variety of circumstances.

Living conditions

If you keep an Italian Greyhound as a pet you will unquestionably have to provide it with a great deal of exercise. Because of its small size, however, it is well suited to live in a flat. If you treat it lovingly and gently this animal will bring you great joy.

The Italian Greyhound develops an easy relationship with its fellow creatures, as well as with children.

Rhodesian Ridgeback

Size and build

This handsome dog stands about 70 cm (28 in) high and weighs 30 to 40 kg (66–88 lb). It has a medium-size head that is not very long, a strong neck and a square body. The sturdy limbs end in round paws.

Coat

Short, glossy, flat hair in all shades ranging from wheat-yellow to reddish brown is typical for the Rhodesian Ridgeback. Dogs of this breed also bear a unique row of bristled hair along its back, from which its name is derived.

Character and disposition

The Rhodesian Ridgeback is an energetic dog, strong-willed with a courageous nature and great endurance.

Living conditions

This dog is primarily used as a hunting dog and to protect farms desian Ridgeback has no trouble getting along with either children or other dogs.

in its native Africa. In fact, its ability to fight lions gave it a second name, the African Lion Dog. It is ideally suited to be a watchdog, a guard dog and a companion dog.

It will best suit this dog's innate qualities if you can provide a house and a garden. The Rho-

Saluki (Gazelle Hound, Persian Greyhound)

Size and build

These fast dogs can grow up to 70 cm (28 in) tall. Their weight is about 20 kg (44 lb). The head of a Saluki is long and narrow. The neck is rather long, as is its back,

and the belly has the tucked up look typical of greyhounds. The Saluki has long, slender, straight limbs.

Coat

The smooth, soft coat is glossy. In some areas, such as the back, among others, the hair may grow longer.

The coat of the Saluki can have various colours and colour combinations, including beige, golden and a shade of red.

Character and disposition

This ancient breed of dog is highly independent and does not readily submit to anybody. It does have a rather gentle nature and tends to be reserved toward strangers.

Living conditions

Sensitivity and tact are essential for successful training of this dignified and intelligent dog.

Bred over thousands of years to run, a Saluki cannot be kept in a flat and it must have many opportunities to exercise.

It is said to have unproblematic relationships both with children and with other dogs.

Whippet

Size and build

The Whippet is visibly smaller than most other windhounds. Attaining a height of around 50 cm (20 in), it weighs only between 10 and 15 kg (22–33 lb).

Although it may be reminiscent of the Greyhound at first sight, the Whippet is rather more delicate.

It has a long head with a strong jaw that tapers markedly toward the front. Its long curved neck flows into the longish back. Its limbs are comparatively slender yet visibly muscular.

Coat

The short, dense coat has a smooth texture, is surprisingly soft to the touch, and comes in several different colours.

Grooming

Taking care of this short smooth coat does not require much work. It is a good idea to wipe down the coat occasionally with a moist cloth.

Character and disposition

These small windhounds have a reputation for being quite undemanding and gentle. If you give the Whippet enough exercise, its disposition will be very well-balanced.

Living conditions

You can keep a Whippet in a moderately sized flat provided that you are prepared to give it plenty of exercise and training.

Since Whippets do not have the most robust constitution it is important that they have a warm and dry home. These dogs get along well with children.

Terriers

Airedale Terrier

Size and build

The Airedale is often called the "king of terriers", and is the tallest of the group, standing about 58 cm (23 in). The "king" weighs only 18 to 25 kg (40–55 lb), however. This dog is powerfully built without being massive.

Coat

The coat of an Airedale should be tan, brown and black. Typical is a saddle-like dark section of the coat on its back extending down to the stomach. The top hair is coarse and hard over a short, soft, woolly undercoat.

Character and disposition

A cheerful, calm disposition is typical for this largest of the terriers. Airedales are devoted, sensitive and uncomplicated and get along with children. In spite of their watchdog qualities, they don't tend to bark without cause.

Living conditions

Airedales can easily be part of a large family. A lot of people and

comparatively small living quarters are not problematic as long as it gets enough activity.

Australian Terrier

Size and build

Strong and sporting very powerful muscles, the Australian

Terrier grows to just 25 cm (10 in) in size, tipping the scales at approximately 4 to 5 kg (9–13 lb). These dogs have a relatively long body and a powerful muzzle.

Coat

The hair on an Australian Terrier's body is long, straight, and wiry.

Around its neck and throat the hair forms a ruff that looks like a mane. The undercoat is shorter and softer. The most popular colourations are blue-black and or silver-black, complemented by tan markings on the legs and head.

Character and disposition

It may come as a surprise given its size, but the Australian Terrier is an extremely courageous dog. They are often described as impetuous, and they will not avoid a fight. On the other hand, they are also known for their devotion. Being of a lively and happy nature, they never get bored.

Living conditions

On account of its size, this small terrier can easily be kept in a flat, and it gets along very well with children. They can be considered family and flat dogs who need regular exercise.

Bedlington Terrier

Size and build

This unusual terrier can reach a height of about 40 cm (16 in) and weighs up to 10 kg (22 lb). It has a sloping rump and its stomach is tucked up like that of a Greyhound.

Coat

These dogs have a thick, woolly top coat and a dense, curly undercoat. White Bedlington Terriers might even be said to resemble sheep! But these dogs also sport other colours.

Character and disposition

Bedlington Terriers are considered rather quiet characters be-

cause they seldom bark. But they are anything but reserved. They are outgoing, independent and playful and often develop great devotion to their owners. Occasionally, however, they tend to be jealous of other pets.

Living conditions

This terrier is a good companion for children, making it a wonderful family dog. A small flat is not the right environment for this dog, as it requires a good deal of exercise. Long walks out of doors do wonders for this dog's well being.

Border Terrier

Size and build

The Border Terrier stands about 30 cm (12 in) tall, usually weighing well under 10 kg (22 lb). This dog has a slender head and a body that is rather square overall, but not very long. Its legs are not too thick. A characteristic trait for this breed—and some others, as well—is its thick, loose skin.

Coat

This terrier's coarse, hard, short hair on top of a thick undercoat protects it from wind, water and inclement weather. Border Terriers are found in several colours, including wheat, red, brown and more, which may be streaked with grey.

Character and disposition

The Border Terrier does not give up very easily: it is persistent. You might even be tempted to call it

obstinate, but it is only fair to acknowledge this animal's great ability to adapt to changing circumstances. In addition, the Border Terrier is lively and fearless.

Living conditions

A Border Terrier will adapt well to a family and is friendly toward children. You shouldn't try to push its adaptable nature too far, however, by forcing it to live in unnatural surroundings. This dog will not enjoy life in a crowded space if you cannot provide it with extended walks in the woods, through fields or other open spaces.

Boston Terrier

Size and build

The Boston Terrier grows to about 30 to 35 cm (12–14 in). Of the

51

three different weight classes, the middle group weighs between 7 and 9 kg (16–20 lb). Their build is robust and strong without being massive. The head is wide and flat with a short muzzle.

Coat

Boston Terriers have short, shiny, soft hair. They should be bi-coloured, either black or seal with white or, better still, a good balance of dark brindle with white markings.

Grooming

It takes little effort to keep the fine, soft hair of a Boston Terrier shining. An occasional brushing of its coat, or wiping it down with a moist rag, is usually sufficient.

Character and disposition

Boston Terriers are ideal companion dogs, combining some very agreeable qualities in their character: they are highly intelligent, lively and clever. In addition, they learn to obey more easily than many dogs.

Living conditions

The Boston Terrier is well suited as a family dog. Its cleverness and fondness for children are advantages in this respect. This moderately-sized dog can also be kept in a flat. Boston Terriers also tend to be watchful, yet without excessive barking.

Bull Terrier

Size and build

There are various sizes of Bull Terriers. The Standard is about 55 cm (22 in) tall, while the smaller class, called a Miniature Bull Terrier, stands less than 36 cm (14 in) high. In general, Bull Terriers should look neither thin nor heavy and immobile. Their physical power should be visible from the overall shape of the animal.

Coat

The coat of this terrier is short, smooth and thick, and the hair

may be white, brindled, or of many colours.

Character and disposition

Unfairly considered by many people to be aggressive, Bull Terriers are in fact very good with people. Their even temperament makes them relatively easy to train, although they may exhibit a certain stubbornness. They make excellent watchdogs.

Living conditions

Bull Terriers as a breed are especially sensitive to the treatment and training they experience. If they are treated badly they will become mean and dangerous, but if they are handled in a firm yet very loving way, Bull Terriers make good family pets. In fact, a Bull Terrier's displays of affection toward its owner can be quite touching. When properly trained, this dog is good with children.

Dandie Dinmont Terrier

Size and build

When fully grown this terrier is between 20 and 30 cm (8–12 in) tall and weighs approximately 8 kg (18 lb). The Dandie Dinmont has an elongated body with very short legs.

Coat

Not "salt and pepper", but "pepper" and "mustard" are the two colour types that can be distinguished with this breed of terrier.

Within each type there are many additional shadings. "Mustard", for example, ranges anywhere from pale yellow to tan and "pepper" comprises shades of grey to black.

Character and disposition

These little dogs have courage and a lot of stamina. In addition, they are highly sociable and exuberantly happy characters.

Living conditions

The Dandie Dimont Terrier is quite a wary dog and tends to be rather suspicious toward all strangers. However, they generally enjoy the company of children and get along well with other dogs. As long as you can take this terrier on many walks and give it exercise, this little bundle of fluff will be quite content to live in a flat.

German Hunting Terrier

Size and build

Dogs of this breed rarely grow taller than 40 cm (16 in) and weigh between 7 and 10 kg (16–22 lb). A square build, medium-length legs and a gaily carried tail give these dogs a sturdy appearance.

Coat

There are shorthaired and wire-haired German Hunting Terriers, both of which have thick coats.

Character and disposition

The German Hunting Terrier is an ardent hunter. This is a decisive, tough and courageous dog that rarely tires.

Living conditions

The German Hunting Terrier really belongs with a hunter. This is one of the few breeds of dog that is not considered suitable as a companion or domestic pet.

Fox Terrier

Size and build

This very popular pet reaches a height of 35 cm to a maximum of 40 cm (14–16 in). Weighing about 8 kg (18 lb) it is relatively light for its stature. Its physique is robust, yet seemingly light. The head is long with a flat skull. The muzzle and the upper part of the head are of approximately the same length.

Coat

There are Smooth and Wirehaired Fox Terriers. The more common wirehaired type has hard, long wiry hair over a soft, dense undercoat.

The smooth type has shorter, flat hair that lies close to the skin. The base colour for a Fox Terrier is always white, with tan and/or black markings.

Character and disposition

Originally bred to hunt down foxes, the Fox Terrier is a courageous and vigilant dog.

It also distinguishes itself with its intelligence, ability to learn, and its desire for human companionship.

Living conditions

The Fox Terrier continues to be used as a hunting dog to the present day, but it is also very popular as a family pet. A house with a garden is a better match for this lively little dog's drive to run about than a flat. In either place, however, you will only have a contented Fox Terrier if you take it on long walks. This breed is reputed to be better behaved toward children than other dogs.

Irish Terrier

Size and build

Dogs of this breed can get to be about 45 cm (18 in) tall and weigh 11 kg (24 lb). Overall they look slender but not slight. The head has an elongated shape and the neck is of medium length. The back is straight and strong. Its legs end in round paws with sturdy pads.

Coat

The top coat of the Irish Terrier is wiry and hard but not too short. The undercoat is short and rather

soft by comparison. Characteristic for this breed is a reddish-brown, yellowish-red or golden colouring.

Character and disposition

The Irish Terrier has a self-confident and proud disposition. If you acknowledge this and treat it accordingly, which means approaching the dog with love and respect, you will find you have a very loyal companion and friend.

These terriers also distinguish themselves with their great courage and boldness and, lest its past as a hunter and watchdog be forgotten, by its attentiveness and vigilance.

Living conditions

If you wish to keep this hunting dog as a pet you will have to provide it with a lot of exercise.

The Irish Terrier's need to move should not be underestimated. It is ideal to keep one in a house with a garden rather than a flat. The Irish Terrier is not always terribly friendly when interacting with other dogs or other small animals, as its hunting instincts are still strong. On the other hand, it gets on with children especially well.

Parson Russell Terrier (Jack Russell Terrier)

Size and build

The Parson Russell Terrier usually stands less than 40 cm (16 in) high, and dogs with shorter legs remain under 30 cm (12 in). Their weight varies accordingly, in the vicinity of 8 kg (18 lb).

Coat

The Parson Russell Terrier has a typical coat pattern consisting of

black, brown or tan-coloured markings on a base coat of white. There are three types of coat: smooth and shorthaired, somewhat longer and roughhaired, and broken-coated, which lies between the other two types.

Character and disposition

These small hunters are intelligent and energetic. They have a joyful, self-confident disposition and are often playful. Typically they are also attentive, watchful and courageous.

Living conditions

Despite its small stature, do not underestimate this busy dog's drive to move about. A Parson Russell Terrier will need a lot of exercise. It gets on well with children and there are usually no problems with other dogs, either.

Kerry Blue Terrier

Size and build

This Irish terrier is not one of the smallest, attaining a height between 45 cm and 50 cm (18–

20 in) and a weight of up to 16 kg (35 lb). It looks robust and compact without appearing over heavy. The long, powerful head has a square muzzle.

The long, strong neck flows into a rather short back. The chest is deep. The front legs are extremely straight and the hind legs are at quite an angle.

Coat

Blue of all shades is the typical colour for the Kerry Blue Terrier. It has a luxurious, silky-soft and curly coat.

Character and disposition

The Kerry Blue Terrier is said to have a certain severity in its disposition, but this is not its only typical trait. This dog is also intelligent, headstrong, vivacious and courageous. It can be very devoted.

Living conditions

Consistent and loving training is especially important with this dog. If you treat it patiently and fairly, you will be rewarded by the very pleasant behaviour of this charming creature.

The Kerry Blue Terrier can get along well with children. Its relationship to other dogs and animals can be tense, although one cannot predict the personality of individual dogs. Wherever you keep this terrier, it needs lots of exercise to feel its best.

Lakeland Terrier

Size and build

This terrier gets to be up to 37 cm (15 in) tall, but at just 8 kg (18 lb) is something of a lightweight. The Lakeland Terrier, a tireless hunter bred in England, has a quite dynamic appearance and a rather slim physique.

Its head is not too long but the muzzle is pronounced. The limbs are sturdy and straight.

Coat

The Lakeland Terrier has a dense and hard top coat above a thick, soft and waterproof undercoat.

The coat comes in a wide range of colours and colour combinations, an especially typical combination being the classic tan with black markings.

Character and disposition

The Lakeland Terrier has a reputation for being a somewhat aggressive dog. But aggression is

59

not its only trait. It can be very playful and vivacious, tireless and is especially attached to its owners, warming up to new people only gradually.

Living conditions

Over time the Lakeland Terrier has progressed from a hunting breed to primarily a pet.

But it has not become purely a companion dog yet. On the contrary, this breed, in particular, requires a lot of activity, and this should be clear to you before you acquire one of these dogs. As a rule, it gets on with other dogs

quite well and has no trouble being around children.

Norwich Terrier

Size and build

This terrier is one of the smallest, stands about 25 cm (10 in) tall and weighs 4 to 5 kg (9–11 lb). It has a rather compact body with a straight back and short limbs. The head is somewhat large in comparison to the body and has a slightly round shape.

Coat

The top coat is wiry and straight over a dense, soft undercoat. The

Norwich Terrier has noticeably longer hair around its neck and shoulders which forms a ruff. There are several different colours, including wheat colour, red and black. Its coat may show streaks of grey, however white markings or patches are not desirable.

Living conditions

If you keep a terrier of this kind in your house you should know that this dog needs a lot of exercise in spite of its small size. The Norwich Terrier is known as a dog that likes children, and also enjoys the companionship of its own kind.

Character and disposition

This breed of terrier is characterised by its spontaneity and high energy level. These are fearless dogs, highly devoted to their masters. Moreover, they are alert and attentive.

Scottish Terrier

Size and build

This well-known terrier with a familiar silhouette stands just 25 to 28 cm (10–11 in) tall and weighs between 8 and 10 kg

(17–22 lb). A Scottish Terrier has a strong trunk and the head is rather large in proportion to the body. The limbs are short and end in good-sized paws.

Coat

Layered over its dense, soft undercoat is a smooth top coat with rather hard hair that is not too short. Very typical for a Scottish Terrier is black or wheat coloured fur, as well as different brindled colours.

Character and disposition

Many pleasant qualities have made the Scottish Terrier a popular pet. These animals are highly intelligent, independent, courageous and very loyal toward their owners. They often treat strangers rather coolly. If they feel threatened they will become unfriendly.

Living conditions

A flat may very well be a suitable space for a terrier of this type and size, if you provide it with enough exercise. The widespread idea that small dogs can do with little exercise is especially not true when it comes to the terrier. As a rule, children will get on well with a Scottish Terrier unless they act too roughly or anxiously with it. The relationship between the Scottish Terrier and other dogs is usually unproblematic.

Staffordshire Bull Terrier

Size and build

This compact and powerful dog grows to be about 35 to 40 cm (14–16 in) tall and weighs between 12 and 16 kg (26– 35 lb). It has a broad head, a short neck and a long back in relation to its height. Its limbs are strong and its paws round.

Coat

The Staffordshire Terrier has glossy, short and smooth hair in many different colours and colour com-

binations, including white, red-brown and blue, as well as combinations with white.

Character and disposition

This kind of dog makes a highly enjoyable pet. They are known for being eager, courageous, brave and active dogs, and they are also very watchful. They are much friendlier toward their masters than toward strangers.

Living conditions

The Staffordshire Terrier is an excellent guard dog. If you want to keep it as a pet, you must make sure it gets enough opportunity to run and exercise. This dog is typically friendly with children, but when dealing with other dogs you may find that it is not always so friendly.

West Highland White Terrier

Size and build

These small terriers can reach a height of about 28 cm (11 in) and weigh from 7 to 10 kg (16–22 lb). The West Highland White Terrier has a round head with a compact jaw. The long neck flows into a stocky trunk. Overall, these dogs have a well-proportioned, rectangular shape and short limbs.

Coat

As its name suggests, this breed should typically have a white coat. The top coat is comparatively long, but of a hard and sleek texture. The soft, dense undercoat lies close to the body.

Character and disposition

This enjoyable little creature is anything but a bore. It is known for its boisterous, playful and pert nature, but it is also easy to train, devoted and loyal.

Living conditions

You can keep the West Highland Terrier easily in a flat if you allow it to have sufficient exercise. These dogs need to be able to romp around. They are not known for being problematic with children or other dogs.

Shepherd Dogs

Appenzell Mountain Dog (Appenzeller Sennenhund)

Size and build

The Appenzell Mountain Dog is one of the smaller of a group of four Swiss working dogs. Muscular without being massive, it stands 48 to 58cm (19–23 in) tall and weighs about 20 kg (44 lb).

Coat

This dog is tricoloured, with russet and yellow markings on a black coat. The front of its chest, part of its face, paws and tip of the tail have white markings.

Character and disposition

There are at least five positive traits for which this dog is known: courage, agility, intelligence, abundant stamina and a watchful nature. The latter trait results in Appenzell Mountain Dogs tending to bark vociferously at strangers.

Suitable surroundings

The Appenzell Mountain Dog is not a city dog. It is most comfortable in a rural setting that affords a lot of space and activity. This animal is especially good with children, putting its herding instincts to use in keeping them out of harm's way.

Bearded Collie (Beardie)

Size and build

This shepherd may grow up to 60 cm (24 in) tall. It has a very long body with a straight back and low-set tail. There is also a somewhat smaller version that weighs about 20 kg (44 lb).

Coat

The Bearded Collie has a soft undercoat covered by wiry hair on top. Various colours can be found, including grey, sandy beige, reddish brown and black.

Character and disposition

The Bearded Collie is known for its gentle and playful nature. It is extremely friendly, with good mental faculties.

Suitable surroundings

The Bearded Collie was bred to be a herding dog and can be trained accordingly. It also makes a wonderful family dog if you give it enough exercise. A house with a garden to run in makes a better home than a large flat. This long-haired collie gets on very well with children.

Bearded Collie

Its body is well-proportioned and compact. Overall, this dog appears relatively tall. Its impressive head bears a powerful muzzle and well-developed jowls.

Bernese Mountain Dog (Berner Sennenhund)

Size and build

This popular Swiss dog may reach a height of 70 cm (28 in) and weighs in at a solid 40 kg (88 lb).

Coat

The coat of this animal is glossy black with a white blaze on the face that extends onto the chest. White-tipped paws are preferred. Touching the coat of a Bernese Mountain Dog is a pleasure. The hair is long and a bit wavy, but not curly. It is clearly shorter on the head than elsewhere on its body.

Character and disposition

Bernese Mountain Dogs combine a whole range of desirable qualities. Their nature is characterised by calm and composure. They are intelligent, eager and attentive. Although they do not tend toward excessive barking, they are watchful and will alert you when strangers approach. These dogs develop great devotion toward "their" humans.

Suitable surroundings

Animals as large as these really ought to have a house and a garden. The Bernese Mountain Dog's need to roam freely is an argument against keeping it in a flat. It enjoys extensive walks. If this Swiss dog is not going to be trained as a guard dog or pro-

tective dog, you will find it also makes an agreeable family dog that will watch over the well being of "his" or "her" family. He will become attached to children, not only getting along with them extremely well, but also guarding and protecting them.

Old English Sheepdog (Bobtail)

Size and build

This large shepherd can reach 65 cm (26 in) tall, and weighs between 30 and 35 kg (66–77 lb). The Bobtail is powerful, yet moves fluidly, with a characteristic bobbing gait at times. Overall, a Bobtail's body is rather compact and the paws are small and round.

Coat

The coat of an Old English Sheepdog is usually the first thing one notices about it. They have an abundance of fur, which is typically long and straight, shaggy and coarse. Underneath that long hair is an undercoat that is resistant to water. Grey or blue with white are the favoured colours.

Character and disposition

Old English Sheepdogs are calm friends and companions. They are also distinguished by their strong loyalty.

Suitable surroundings

A vital condition for this dog is a lot of space. If an Old English Sheepdog lives in a flat you must make sure it gets sufficient exercise, which it genuinely needs to remain healthy. These heepdogs make good family pets. They enjoy children, who are comfortable around them because these dogs are not easily flustered or agitated.

Like all sheepdogs, they were bred for herding sheep and they need to be kept busy with purposeful activity. Lying around doing nothing all day is not appropriate for these working dogs.

Border Collie

Size and build

This renowned sheep herding dog is usually about 50 cm (20 in) high at the shoulder and weighs around 20 kg (44 lb). An athletic and well proportioned creature, it has a strong back and chest with a gracefully curving tail.

Coat

It comes in a variety of colours, all of which are acceptable so long as white does not predominate. The coat is short or moderately long-haired. Longhaired dogs should have feathered breeching, a mane and a bushy tail.

Character and disposition

A Border Collie quickly understands what you want from it,

67

and reacts speedily. Known for their endless energy and intelligence, they are very lively dogs and show great devotion to their owners.

Suitable surroundings

Border Collies get along particularly well with children. This attribute in combination with their superior obedience and loyalty make them well-suited to be family dogs. They do need access to the outdoors, however, and should definitely not be kept in a cramped flat.

Briard (Berger de Brie)

Size and build

The Briard is a fairly large shepherd, standing almost 70 cm (28 in) tall and weighing approximately 30 kg (66 lb). This dog has a straight back, muscular limbs and a large head.

Coat

The Briard typically has dry and pliable hair which is about 7 cm (3 in) long, wavy, and spread evenly all over its body. This dog's

fur should be of one colour, but not white.

Character and disposition

The Briard is gentle and sensitive, not at all timid and highly courageous. They have often been used as watch dogs.

Suitable surroundings

A small flat is not a suitable home for a Briard, but a larger flat is acceptable.

As with any longhaired dog, you should consider whether the hair that it will shed—in spite of regular brushing—will be too much of a nuisance. The Briard not only needs space, it also needs a tremendous level of activity. It gets on very well with other dogs and with children.

Collie (Scottish Collie)

Size and build

This beloved breed reaches a height of about 60 cm (24 in) and weighs about 20 kg (44 lb). There is no difference in build between the Rough (longhaired) Collie and the smooth, shorthaired form, even though they look very different at first glance because of their strikingly different coats. Collies are very slender in comparison to other herding dogs and they do not appear massive.

Coat

The hair of the longhaired type feels softer at the tips than at the roots, and it is especially long on the throat and chest.

The shorthaired version has a short, dense coat; the hair lies flat and close to the dog's skin. Collies come in a tricoloured (black, white and tan) variation, amongst others, or they can be white and sandy coloured.

Character and disposition

The Collie is a particularly joyful character, yet is also calm and dignified. It learns quite readily, but its great merits will not come to the fore unless it is treated sensitively.

Suitable surroundings

It is no problem for the Collie to be kept as a household pet. Occasionally it will not get along with other dogs even though it does exceptionally well with children. You should, however, keep in mind that this dog was bred to herd sheep, a task that requires a lot of running. Even as a pet the Collie will still need much exercise.

German Shepherd (Alsatian)

Size and build

A fully grown German Shepherd stands about 60 to 65 cm (24–26 in) tall at the shoulder and weighs up to 40 kg (88 lb). The body is somewhat elongated, with a strong throat and a muscular and well-proportioned physique. The head is slim and narrow with a fairly long and powerful muzzle. The lips lie close to the teeth. Ears are medium-sized, pointed and erect.

Coat

German Shepherds are found in shorthaired, wirehaired and long-

haired varieties. The coat can have various colours and shades, often with markings. The following combinations are widespread: red-brown, tan with a black saddle, entirely black, ash grey and iron grey. A so-called "wolf's coat" has various dark shades throughout.

Character and disposition

One of the most popular dogs the world over, the German Shepherd combines several desirable qualities in its character. It is energetic, courageous and vigilant, as well as willing and very able to learn things quickly. If it is not trained or treated well, it can develop an aggressive and tough demeanor.

Suitable surroundings

Thorough training, plenty of activity and lots of space are the three things that will make the German Shepherd a valuable and contented canine partner. A house with a garden is a prerequisite, and this dog should have some kind of task to perform. As they don't bark excessively, they can theoretically be kept in a flat—if you can provide enough exercise and activity. German Shepherds can develop good relationships with other dogs and children. As with other breeds, however, the sooner the dog gets used to children the better its relationship with them will be.

Komondor

Size and build

This striking Hungarian dog is quite large, up to 80 cm (32 in) tall and 50 kg (110 lb). A strong, muscular dog, it has a medium-sized head with a rather wide muzzle. The neck flows into a comparatively short back. The Komondor has sturdy limbs and large paws.

Coat

Anyone who has ever genuinely observed a Komondor will remember the sight: its unique coat is its most characteristic trait. A Komondor's hair is extremely long, corded and matted together. This extravagant coat doesn't fully develop until a dog is three to four years old. The colour of the Komondor is white, although it may not be a pure white, but a somewhat warmer shade.

Bred to guard herds of sheep even in the absence of its master, this coat protected the dogs and helped them blend in with the flocks.

Character and disposition

A Komondor does not stand for any nonsense. Its most dominant trait is watchfulness, and most of the time it is rather reserved toward anyone unfamiliar. A Komondor is a dog that maintains its independence and will not tolerate any unfair treatment. If this dog is treated with respect it will develop tremendous loyalty toward its master.

Suitable surroundings

If you are looking for a family dog to cuddle and play with in your home, this is almost certainly not the dog for you. This is especially true if you have lively children in the household, as the Komondor is not known for its friendliness toward children.

Bred at one time to defend sheep from predators, this large dog thrives when it has a task and is thus especially well-suited to be a guard dog.

Space to move about is an essential prerequisite for the Komondor's well-being. You should only keep this unique dog if you can offer it sufficient room in a house with a sizeable garden.

Belgian Shepherd Dogs

Size and build

The most widely known Belgian shepherd dogs are the Groenendael, Laekenois, Malinois and Tervuren. There are less common varieties of Belgian shepherds, as well, such as the Belgian Herdshond. All of them are approximately the same size and have a slim build. They reach a height of about 70 cm (28 in) and weigh no more than 30 kg (66 lb).

Coat

The Groenendael has a characteristic longhaired, black coat while the Laekenois has wiry, yellow hair streaked with black or grey. Malinois (pictured, opposite) are shorthaired and yellow, with a black face mask and markings on various parts of the body. Tervurens also have a black mask but paired with a long, mahogany coat. Groenedaels and Tervurens have a ruff of long hair around their necks.

Character and disposition

Belgian shepherd dogs are very active. They pay close attention to what is happening around them, but they do not act purely on impulse. They are also highly sensitive animals and may seem to be nervous. They learn easily and adapt well to changes in their surroundings.

Suitable surroundings

The lively, delicate nature of Belgian Shepherds combined with their eagerness to learn prescribes their ideal living situation: they thrive when someone teaches them what is expected and required of them. A Belgian Shepherd can adapt to many situations, but should not be kept in a flat without a lot of exercise. They require substantial activity and love to have something to do. Under appropriate circumstances, you can expect these large dogs to get on very well with children.

Bergamasco (Pastore Bergamasco)

Size and build

This sturdy, well-proportioned sheepdog may be 60 cm (24 in) tall, and is not a lightweight. It will weigh about 30 to 35 kg (66–77 lb) when full grown.

Coat

The Bergamasco has an abundance of hair. An oily undercoat protects it from wind and rain

73

and the top coat is long and shaggy, wavy around the face and distinctively corded on much of the body and legs. The coat may be any variation of grey, with or without white markings.

Character and disposition

Bergamascos are smart dogs—they combine intelligence with flexibility. Courage, liveliness and sociability make them wonderful companions.

Suitable surroundings

The Bergamasco is decidedly not a dog for a flat. Its nature is as rugged as its coat. If you live in the city with a Bergamasco, you will need to organise frequent trips out into the country. This dog needs a vast amount of exercise.

Hungarian Puli (Puli)

Size and build

Like the Komondor, the Puli is a Hungarian herding dog. It will grow up to 45 cm (18 in) tall and weigh between 10 and 15 kg (22–33 lb). Under a mass of unusual hair, its small head has a short round muzzle.

Coat

The long coat of the Puli can reach all the way to the ground. It is shaggy and may have different qualities depending on the composition of the top and undercoats. It is desirable for the coat to become matted and form long cords. The typical colours are solid black with red highlights as well as several shades of white and grey.

Character and disposition

In spite of its almost comical appearance, the Puli is no slouch; quite the opposite: this is an energetic, active and eager dog. It is known as a dog that maintains its independence.

Suitable surroundings

A Puli will be more comfortable in a house with a garden rather than a city flat—unless you are able to provide it with tremendous exercise in the city.

This dog is known for its friendliness toward children, though mistrustful of strangers. It is uncomplicated with other dogs.

Rottweiler

Size and build

This dog is increasingly popular as a companion dog. It can be up to 70 cm (28 in) tall and weigh between 40 and 60 kg (88–132 lb). A massive, powerful dog, the Rottweiler has a broad skull, a muscular neck and a deep chest.

Coat

The coat of the Rottweiler is hard and short and lies close to the skin. It is always black, with tan or mahogany markings. Markings above the eyes, on the cheeks, muzzle and chest, as well as on the legs are desirable.

Character and disposition

Intelligent, courageous and robust, the Rottweiler also stands out for its devotion to its family. This breed has historically served as a guard and patrol dog, and still has a strong tendency toward protective behaviour.

Suitable surroundings

A Rottweiler can be used as a working dog in several different situations. If you keep it as a companion dog, not surprisingly it will be more comfortable in a house with a garden rather than a flat. Its relationship with children is, on the whole, quite unproblematic. Exercise and purposeful activity as well as fair and consistent training and stable ownership are important so that dog and owner can develop a strong bond.

Shetland Sheepdog (Sheltie)

Size and build

These dogs can grow up to 37 cm (15 in) tall and reach a weight of about 8 kg (17 lb). In almost all of their traits, Shelties look like miniature Rough Collies. The head is long with a tapered muzzle and the legs are straight.

Coat

The Sheltie's top coat is long and smooth, while the undercoat is soft and dense. The Sheltie may have a coat that is all one colour, or it can sport two or three colours. The characteristic tricolour combination is white with black and tan.

Character and disposition

The Sheltie is known to have a lively, intelligent nature and is eager to please. This is a patient and undemanding dog. A Sheltie can develop great devotion toward its master, but more often than not will behave cautiously around strangers.

Suitable surroundings

The Sheltie is a shepherd. If you keep it as a pet you will have to provide plenty of space for the dog to run around, so that it can let off some steam. Shelties are

77

known to like children and their relationship with other dogs is unproblematic.

Tibetan Terrier

Size and build

This Asian dog can grow to be as large as 40 cm (16 in) tall and can weigh up to 15 kg (33 lb). It has a very compact physique with a medium length skull, a straight back and quite solid legs.

Coat

The unique, shaggy look of this dog makes a memorable impression when one first encounters the breed. Originally bred in the harsh climate of the Himalayans, it has a long, smooth but wavy top coat with a soft texture. The undercoat is also soft and woolly. The coat of the Tibetan Terrier comes in a variety of colours and colour combinations, including white and black as well as shades of grey and gold.

Character and disposition

The Tibetan Terrier is known for its intelligence and self assurance. It shows a great deal of devotion toward its master but is very reserved around strangers. This breed is remarkably attentive and watchful.

Suitable surroundings

A house with a garden is more suitable to the Tibetan Terrier's nature than a small flat since this dog requires lots of exercise. Be-

cause the animal's devotion does not have to be limited to only one person, this breed makes an excellent family dog. If it is to be a family dog, one should expose it to children as early in the dog's life as possible, advice that holds for many other breeds as well.

Welsh Corgi

Size and build

These rather short-legged shepherds come in two types, the Welsh Corgi Cardigan and the Welsh Corgi Pembroke. Welsh Corgi Cardigans can grow up to about 30 cm (12 in) and weigh 12 kg (26 lb). The Welsh Corgi Pembroke may be a bit smaller, standing 25 to 30 cm (10–12 in) and weighing less—about 8 to 12 kg (17–26 lb). The Welsh Corgi has a longish rectangular shape with a strong trunk and short limbs. Its head is relatively large in relation to its body, with large upright ears. The muzzle and jaw are long, calling to mind the shape of a fox's head.

At first sight, the Welsh Corgi Cardigan and the Welsh Corgi Pembroke are not easy to distinguish from one another, but if you look closely you will recognize some subtle differences, such as the fact that the body of the Welsh Corgi Pembroke has a less cylindrical shape.

Coat

The Welsh Corgi Cardigan has short or long smooth hair in a number of different colours and colour combinations, but may not be pure white. The Welsh Corgi Pembroke, on the other hand, has a coat of slightly hard texture and medium length. Typical colour combinations include browns of many shades, white and black.

Character and disposition

These small dogs are very attentive. Nothing escapes them. They are quite willing to learn, they are intelligent, and they adapt very well to changing circumstances.

Suitable surroundings

The Welsh Corgi can easily be kept in a city flat assuming it gets enough exercise. These animals are known to have a good relationship with children. This and their adaptability make these dogs great family pets.

Danes and Mastiffs

Saint Bernard

Size and build

The Saint Bernard was never intended to be a small animal. This powerful dog should attain a height of no less than 65 to 70 cm (26–28 in) when fully grown, and 70 cm (28 in) is considered the minimum for a male. A large Saint Bernard weighs up to an impressive 90 kg (198 lb). This dog has a broad back and chest, and the legs are muscular.

Coat

There are long- and shorthaired Saint Bernards (or rough- and smoothcoated). The former does not have extremely long hair, but

it is of medium length and can be a bit wavy. The shorthaired type has noticeably shorter and coarser—but not wiry—hair that lies close to the skin. Typical colours are red, mahogany and orange with white. A Saint Bernard should have white markings at least around the nose, throat, chest, paws and tail.

Character and disposition

The Saint Bernard has a friendly and calm disposition. But that is not the end of their positive qualities: their exceptional intelligence, reliability and devotion have to be mentioned as well.

Living conditions

Saint Bernards are not lazy dogs. They do enjoy a certain amount of lounging about, but they also need movement. Exercise gives them an opportunity to show off their strength and stamina. Not surprisingly, a dog of this stature will not do well in a small flat. A home with a garden is a more appropriate fit.

Great Dane (German Mastiff)

Size and build

These imposing dogs can and should be tall; a height of about

80 cm (32 in) is not at all rare. They weigh approximately 54 to 60 kg (118–132 lb). A Great Dane has a strong back, powerful legs and a rather long head.

Coat

The coat of a Great Dane is dense and short. The hair is glossy and lies close to the skin.

There are a number of colours, some of which fall into separate types. The Harlequin Great Dane, for example, with its white coat and irregular dark patches, is distinct from solid coloured or brindled Great Danes.

Character and disposition

The Great Dane is loyal to its owner, but suspicious toward strangers. One of the remarkable traits of this ancient breed is its watchfulness. Contrary to what one might expect, it is otherwise a rather calm animal.

Living conditions

A house with a garden is really the minimum space you need to keep this large beast successfully; in fact, this is one of the breeds that one is advised to keep as an outside dog. These fast animals need a lot of exercise. If a Great Dane is trained with love and a

firm hand, you will find that they can develop very trusting relationships with children.

Boxer
(German Boxer)

Size and build

This easily recognisable dog gets to be about 60 cm (24 in) high. It is hardly a lightweight at 25 to 30 kg (55–66 lb), but is also not extremely heavy for its size. Overall the Boxer gives the impression of being a very powerful dog. It has a striking head with a short muzzle, an overbite and fleshy upper lips. The neck is muscular without dewlaps. It has a deep chest and the back slopes slightly toward the rear.

Coat

The Boxer's coat is short, smooth and shiny. You will find them in a variety of colours from red-brown to almost yellow, one uniform colour or brindled. Boxers may have some white markings, but they should not predominate, and any stripes should not be too wide.

Character and disposition

The Boxer is a very passionate animal. With loving and patient training it can learn how to use its power without disturbing its owner. Individuals well-suited for breeding are distinguished especially by their even temperament and favourable qualities including courage, reliability and loyalty.

Living conditions

If you are looking for a watchdog, a Boxer is an excellent choice because they have so much courage that they won't back down

from anything. Apart from that, they also make wonderful family pets. They get along extremely well with children, who can have a lot of fun romping around with this dog. If getting more exercise yourself is a factor in your decision for a specific breed, you can keep a Boxer in a flat. You and the

dog can then tire yourselves out on lengthy walks. Because this is such an energetic animal you will want to make sure that you provide it with enough positive outlets for that energy through activity.

Dogue de Bordeaux (French Mastiff)

Size and build

This dog is anything but small. A French Mastiff can reach a height of 70 cm (28 in) and weighs 50 kg (110 lb) and up. French Mastiffs have a large, powerful head, in keeping with their overall muscular build.

Coat

This heavy animal has a short and silky coat. The hair may be a number of shades of yellow, mahogany and brown.

Character and disposition

The French Mastiff's massive appearance might easily lead to the assumption that they tend to brutality. Though this ancient dog was once bred to fight, that is not the case anymore. As long as this dog is raised with a great deal of love and patience it will become very friendly, even gentle, and is highly devoted to its owners.

Living conditions

A large, powerful dog requires a lot of space, and this holds true for the French Mastiff as well.

Keeping a French Mastiff without a garden is a bad idea. If properly trained, they can be excellent watchdogs.

The brawny exterior of this gentle giant is deceptive, because when it is raised in a proper environment it develops loving relationships with children, even to the extent of protecting them.

Bulldog (English Bulldog)

Size and build

These small but powerful dogs can get up to 40 cm (16 in) tall. With a weight of about 25 kg (55 lb) they are comparatively heavy. They have a massive head and characteristic pendulous upper lips.

The body is stout and tapers toward the back, which in combination with the large head size occasionally causes problems for the females when giving birth.

Coat

The Bulldog's coat is short, soft and dense. Several colours are permissible, including fawn and shades of red, as well as brindled variations.

Character and disposition

This animal may not have the friendliest appearance, but in this case looks can be deceptive. In fact, when properly raised, Bulldogs are gentle, friendly and adorable companion dogs. They are reliable and devoted to their owners, and very watchful in addition.

Living conditions

A Bulldog does not need a lot of exercise, at least in comparison with other dogs. They are said to be extremely good with children. Their behaviour toward other animals, however, may sometimes be aggressive.

Fila Brazileiro (Brazilian Mastiff)

Size and build

This dog is neither small nor a lightweight. Fully grown it stands up to 75 cm (30 in) tall and can weigh more than 50 kg (110 lb). It looks decidedly powerful: the back is strong, rising slightly to the rump. Its limbs are large and thick, right down to the toes. The head is rather large with a blunt muzzle.

Coat

The coat is thick, short and soft. The typical colouring is in the yellow-brown range, either one solid colour or brindled. White markings can be found, as well.

Character and disposition

This dog won't stand for any nonsense if it does not know you. The Fila Brasileiro can develop great affection for its master, but toward strangers it can often show its quite natural aggressive tendencies.

Living conditions

The Fila Brasileiro cannot be considered an appropriate pet in the usual sense: it can become too aggressive. Bred by colonists in Brazil and used for many tasks, it is more in keeping with its nature to keep this dog for hunting or as a watchdog.

Working with an expert trainer, however, this dog has the potential to become a loving and irreplaceable friend. It is largely up to the owner what will become of this dog. Great caution is called for when children are around, especially unfamiliar children. The Fila Brasileiro is also not very compatible with other dogs.

Hovawart

Size and build

This breed, which was already known during the Middle Ages, can get up to 70 cm (28 in) in height and can weigh up to 40 kg (88 lb). Hovawarts have a well-proportioned and strong-looking physique in rectangular form. The head is large with a strong muzzle. The medium-long neck is also quite strong and flows into the solid back.

The front legs are powerful, the hind legs well-muscled. The legs end in sturdy paws.

Coat

The Hovawart has a straight or slightly wavy—but never curly—top coat which is a bit coarse. The undercoat is somewhat dense.

Longer, thicker hair can be found at the neck, the back of the legs and on the feathered tail.

The colours black and yellow are typical for Hovawarts.

Character and disposition

Hovawarts are courageous and reliable, but have a quiet and patient way about them as well. They stand out for their intelligence and ability to learn.

They can develop great devotion for their owners. Hovawarts retain their youthful playfulness for quite some time.

Living conditions

A house, possibly even a farmhouse on a large plot of land, is a good place for a Hovawart. Lots of outdoor exercise is good for it and bad weather doesn't faze this dog in the least. It's an excellent runner who does well even in rough terrain.

As with many other breeds, it is a good idea to make use of the dog's capabilities. In this case, the Hovawart makes an ideal watchdog on a large property. If it recognizes danger it will avert it with constant barking.

With its quiet, patient manner the Hovawart gets on with children, as well as with other dogs.

Hungarian Kuvasz (Kuvasz)

Size and build

This Hungarian working dog, developed many centuries ago, can reach a height of 75 cm (29 in) and weighs approximately 50 kg (110 lb). It has a harmonious build which looks powerful to heavy, but not without a certain elegance. The head has a longish shape and the muzzle tapers a bit toward the front without being pointed. The Kuvasz has muscular limbs.

Coat

This dog should be white to ivory coloured with no markings. Its coat is of medium length and

87

very luxurious. It may lie flat or be wavy, and feels a bit coarse and rough to the touch. The hair is somewhat shorter on the paws, head and on the ears.

Living conditions

While it is adaptable enough to be kept as a companion rather than a guardian, this is no dog for a flat in the city. A spacious house

Kuvasz gets on well with children and has no problems with other dogs.

Leonberger

Size and build

Bred to resemble a lion in the seal of the German town of Leonberg, the Leonberger is undeniably impressive and dignified. It stands

with a big garden or a farm is the environment in which a Kuvasz will thrive. It will also happily take on the role of a watchdog. Generous opportunities to run and exercise are absolutely necessary for its well-being. As a rule, the

up to 80 cm (32 in) and easily weighs 60 kg (132 lb). Its head is rather like that of a Saint Bernard, but a bit slimmer and not as high. The neck is slightly arched and the back moderately long. The powerful limbs end in round,

closed paws, often with webbed toes which help them swim.

Coat

These dogs have a dense, rather long top coat which usually lies close to the skin, but may stand out somewhat. The undercoat is also dense.

A typical and especially popular colour combination in the Leonberger is golden-brown to chestnut-brown, preferably with the black mask that is a signature of this breed. Other colours are found frequently as well. The tips of individual hairs may be darker or black, no matter what the base colour of the coat.

Character and disposition

The Leonberger is a reliable and good-natured dog. It is characterised by its intelligence, the ability to learn and a calm, gentle

disposition. This dog is friendly and affectionate toward its family, and will take on the role of protector. It does tend to be reserved toward strangers.

Living conditions

The Leonberger fills a variety of functions in its primary capacity as a working dog. It makes a fine rescue dog, for example.

If you want to keep one as a pet, you will have to provide it with a lot of room. While this dog isn't a great runner or racer, it still needs regular long walks—and on account of its size alone—a lot of space.

The Leonberger is known to be good with children.

Mastiff

Size and build

This unusually massive dog can reach a height of about 80 cm (32in). Its weight usually ranges between 70 and 90 kg (154–198 lb).

It has extremely powerful limbs ending in round paws. The body has a square shape overall; the head is wide with a powerful and broad muzzle.

Coat

The Mastiff has a short, smooth coat which may be a variety of colours, especially shades of golden yellow and red. The coat may be brindled as well. The ears and nose should be black.

Character and disposition

In its current form, the Mastiff is considered not only very good natured and peaceful toward people it trusts, but is also very affectionate.

It can also be unpleasant, ready to attack and dangerous toward strangers if it gets excited.

Living conditions

Mastiffs have been guard dogs and hunters for more than two thousand years, and some are still trained as watchdogs or protective dogs today.

This dog requires a lot of space and activity. They are gentle with children that they know and like. They seek out human contact, and the owner of a Mastiff must be prepared to invest a great deal of time in the relationship.

A Mastiff belongs with experienced and highly responsible dog owners.

Neapolitan Mastiff (Mastino)

Size and build

The Neapolitan Mastiff stands approximately 70 cm (28 in) tall and weighs 50 to 70 kg (110–154 lb). It has a very powerful body with a wide head and a very strong jaw. The plentiful loose folds of skin around the throat, called a dewlap, are characteristic of the breed.

Coat

The coat of this dog is extremely short and lies close to the body. Grey, black and yellow are some of the most common colours. The coat may be all one colour or brindled and should be glossy.

Character and disposition

This dog is distinguished by its self-confidence. It has a tendency to be aggressive. Whether the dog behaves peacefully depends to a large extent on its training.

Living conditions

In addition to space and a lot of exercise, training is of great importance with this breed. It is essential to foster friendly behaviour by being loving but firm from a young age. This dog will bond strongly with one person.

The Neapolitan Mastiff is not a dog for someone without a lot of prior experience with dogs. This animal needs to be in the hands of an experienced owner who can establish a good relationship between owner and dog.

This dog is an excellent choice to train as a guard dog and for personal protection. When dealing with children, however, caution is advised. The Neapolitan Mastiff will often try to dominate other dogs.

Newfoundland

Size and build

This dog, also called a Newfie, is an impressive sight. The Newfoundland can reach a height of up to 70 cm (28 in) and can weigh about 70 kg (154 lb). It has a powerful and very solid build, but does not seem to be heavy. Its limbs are strong and it has the webbed paws typical of dogs bred to work in water. Its back is broad and straight and the neck strong. The head of a Newfoundland is wide with a comparatively short muzzle covered with shorter fur.

93

Coat

A dense, long and rugged top coat is layered over the softer, water-resistant undercoat.

The Newfoundland is not a particularly colourful dog: typical coats are black, brown or white. Markings may or may not be present.

Character and disposition

This dog is known to have a host of lovely qualities. It is loyal, peaceful and good-natured. It responds well to training and can be taught many things.

Living conditions

It goes without saying that a dog of this size is not suitable for a small flat. You should at least be able to provide it with a house with a garden. The Newfoundland loves water. You will make it very happy by taking it on long walks that pass by one or two sources of cool water. The Newfoundland can be very patient with children.

Pyrenean Mountain Dog (Great Pyrenees)

Size and build

This pastoral dog, which has been bred to guard livestock from pre-dators in the Pyrenees Mountains for thousands of years, grows up to 80 cm (32 in) tall and carries a proud weight of 50 kg (110 lb) and more. The Great Pyrenees is an impressive sight with a strong, slightly elongated body and a well-proportioned head.

Coat

All white or white with rather light markings are typical coat colours for the Pyrenean.

Its hair is dense, medium-length and lies almost flat, though it may be slightly wavy. Longer hair grows around the neck and on the tail.

Character and disposition

This large and powerful dog is known to be well balanced with a tendency toward independence. It is also an alert and protective watchdog.

Living conditions

A small flat in the city is not the right environment for the Pyrenean Mountain Dog.

It will be much more satisfied if it's given plenty of space and a task. Its gentle disposition is a good foundation for getting along well with children.

Toy Dogs

Affenpinscher

Size and build

A genuine leightweight, Affenpinschers can reach 28 cm (11 in) in height and weigh up to 4 kg (9 lb).

Coat

This little pinscher is typically black. There are other colours, such as grey or red, though they are not as desirable according to the standard. The coat is dry, coarse, long and thick with a fluffy undercoat.

Character and disposition

Alert and watchful, boredom is sure to dissipate with one of these dogs around, because they are lively and vivacious. Their great devotion toward their owners is a distinctive trait.

Living conditions

An Affenpinscher can be kept in a city flat, provided it is given regu-

lar opportunities to exercise, of course. They are well-suited to be family dogs and will establish a distinct relationship with each member of the family.

Bolognese (Bichon Bolognese)

Size and build

The Bolognese grows to be about 30 cm (12 in) tall and weighs between 3 and 5 kg (7–11 lb). The height of the shoulders corresponds with that of the trunk.

Coat

This little dog's hair is reminiscent of a Poodle's and should be pure white. The coat feels fluffy and silky. The hair on the ears and on the tail is somewhat longer.

Character and disposition

This small companion dog is not especially active; in fact, you could even call it rather calm. It develops great devotion toward its owner.

Living conditions

Because of its size and disposition, this dog is quite content living in a flat. As is true of all dogs, naturally it needs some exercise. The Bolognese is certainly not un-friendly toward children, but cannot be expected to romp around and play with them, either. It is very important for this animal to have one continuous person in its life with whom it can form a close bond. A Bolognese will always be most comfortable when that person is around.

Bichon Frisé (Tenerife Dog)

Size and build

Standing just 30 cm (12 in) tall when it is fully grown, this slight Mediterranean dog weighs 4 kg (9 lb) or less. It has dark, round eyes and pendant ears.

Coat

White is the favoured colour for the Bichon Frisé, though it may have brown or grey spots.

Character and disposition

This bichon is an attentive, quick learning, lively animal much like its relatives. Another typical quality is its devotion to its human companions.

Living conditions

A Bichon Frisé makes a lovely family dog. It gets along famously with children, and because of its petite size it can be kept even in a small flat. Bichons require less activity than many other dogs.

Havanese (Bichon Havanais)

Size and build

This small Mediterranean dog reaches a maximum height of 25 to 35 cm (10–14 in) and weighs up to 6 kg (13 lb). It has a longish silhouette with rather short legs.

The chest is deep with a wide ribcage, and the rump slopes slightly.

Coat

A long, soft and primarily straight coat distinguishes the Havanese. Only the tips of the hair may be a little wavy. Typical for this breed are lighter colours such as grey, gold, beige and less frequently white, but all shades of brown, and even spotted coats, also occur.

Character and disposition

"Good things come in small packages" can be said about the Havanese. It is a lively, loyal companion dog who loves to play and learn tricks.

Living conditions

This kind of dog does not require a large garden. You still need to provide enough opportunity for movement, but the Havanese is one of the breeds that is well suited to live in a city.

It is also very convenient that in general the Havanese doesn't bark excessively. It gets on with other dogs very well, and possibly even better with children.

Maltese

Size and build

The Maltese, perhaps the oldest toy breed, stands about 25 cm (10 in) when fully grown and

weighs just 3 to 4 kg (6–9 lb). It has an elongated, not especially delicate body, slender neck and a round head with pointed muzzle.

Coat

The coat of the Maltese is certainly eye-catching: the hair is long, straight, soft and grows in abundance. The preferred colour is pure white.

Character and disposition

This small creature is vivacious, clever and playful. In addition to that it loves to cuddle.

Living conditions

A Maltese can be kept in the smallest flat. It is amiable with dogs and quite friendly toward children.

Lowchen (Little Lion Dog)

Size and build

Fully grown, this small dog stands only 30 cm (12 in) high and weighs about 4 kg (9 lb). It has traits typical of a bichon and appears to be almost square, with a tail that curves up over its back.

Coat

The coat is quite long, wavy and soft and may be of any colour.

Especially typical, however, are white, black and a pale yellow.

Character and disposition

This companion breed is vivacious, clever and devoted to its people.

Living conditions

Owing to its small size, the Little Lion Dog is content in a flat.

Cavalier King Charles Spaniel

Size and build

This miniature spaniel stands no more than 35 cm (14 in) high and as a rule weighs less than 8 kg (17 lb). It has a sturdy trunk and well-proportioned legs.

Coat

This native English spaniel has a long, soft, silky hair that may be wavy, but not curly. The various colourings that occur in Cavalier King Charles Spaniels—combinations of black, tan, white and chestnut—have distinct names such as Blenheim (chestnut with white), for example, and Prince Charles (tricolour).

Character and disposition

The Cavalier King Charles Spaniel is not a wallflower. It loves to play

and is very lively and sociable. Furthermore, it can adapt easily to new situations and is said to be quite obedient. This confluence of traits made the Cavalier King Charles Spaniel a favourite with nobility, and they were often featured in portraits together with their masters.

Living conditions

Any miniature spaniel can be at home in a city flat, but of course it will need exercise, as is true for most dogs. It can expend some of its energy by romping about in the garden and develops a good relationship with children.

Chihuahua

Size and build

The smallest of all breeds, the Chihuahua is a tiny, lightweight dog that rarely grows taller than 20 cm (8 in) and only weighs between 1 and 3 kg (2–7 lb).

Coat

There are longhaired and short-haired types. In this breed all colours and colour combinations are acceptable.

Character and disposition

In spite of its diminutive size, the Chihuahua is watchful, fearless

101

and overall a rather lively dog. Intelligent and obedient, this is the ultimate lapdog—it seems to live just to be part of the action and be coddled.

Living conditions

Even a small flat offers enough space for this dog, and it doesn't require much exercise. Chihuahuas tend to have no fear of other dogs, even when that might be warranted. They need a generous amount of attention and do very well with children.

Coton de Tuléar

Size and build

This little companion dog looks similar to the Maltese, but comes from the island of Madagascar. When full grown it stands about 30 cm (12 in) tall and usually weighs around 4 kg (9 lb).

Coat

The long hair of the Coton de Tuléar, which is most often pure white, feels just like cotton—hence the name.

Character and disposition

The Coton de Tuléar is a very vivacious and intelligent, even spirited dog. Developing a loyal and loving relationship with its owner is the strength of this dog.

Living conditions

Even though this dog is small and otherwise well-suited for a flat, it feels even more at home in a house with a garden. The Coton de Tuléar gets along well with other dogs, even larger ones, and also with children. Indeed, this is a highly sociable dog. With good consistent training, this breed will feel right at home in a busy household with many people and even with other pets.

Japanese Chin

Size and build

Members of this ancient breed, venerated in Japan, are extreme-ly small. They reach a height of about 20 to 25 cm (8–10 in), with a maximum weight of just 3 kg (6.5 lb).

Coat

Supple, silky hair is a typical trait of the Japanese Chin. The coat stands out a bit from its body. Especially striking is the mass of hair around its neck. The coat is characteristically white with black or red to golden red markings.

The chest area and around the muzzle should always be white.

Character and disposition

This diminutive toy dog is lively, friendly and clever. It likes to play and is very devoted to its owners. But you should not think of it only

as a playful fellow because it can also be quite watchful.

Living conditions

A Japanese Chin can easily be kept in a flat and will be very happy there as long as you pay it enough attention and take the dog with you as often as possible. A Chin enjoys children and other dogs, but keep in mind that it is a somewhat fragile creature.

King Charles Spaniel

Size and build

As its name suggests, this toy spaniel is very similar to the Cavalier King Charles. The King Charles looks somewhat more robust than its cousin.

Coat

As with the Cavalier King Charles Spaniel, there are several typical colours and combinations of the colours white, red, black and tan that have specific names (see page 100) for these breeds. Regardless of colour, the coat is dense and the hair is long, silky and slightly wavy.

Character and disposition

A King Charles Spaniel will seldom give you any trouble in the home. This very sociable lap dog is sweet, gentle and affectionate with its owner. But it is far from boring; it is happy, intelligent and quite playful.

Living conditions

The King Charles Spaniel has been an exceptionally popular pet for centuries. Because of its small size it can be kept in a city flat and requires less opportunity to run and exercise than many other dogs.

If the dog is shut into a small space with nothing to do it will not be content and will not be enjoyable to anybody around it.

In general, this dog is extremely friendly toward other dogs and gets on very well with children.

Lhasa Apso

Size and build

This ancient Tibetan toy breed generally doesn't get much taller than 25 cm (10 in) and it weighs between 5 and 7 kg (11–16 lb). It has a relatively long body. The neck is strong and not too short. The head is slim with a medium-length muzzle. The paws are distinctly round.

Coat

The Lhasa Apso has a characteristic luxurious, rather long coat that falls away from a parting down its back. The hair is not soft, as one might expect, but rather hard and straight.

There is more than one typical coat colouration. One frequently sees golden and lion coloured, but there are also various shades of grey and even multicoloured animals.

Character and disposition

This dog distinguishes itself with its affection for people, combined with a calm and self-confident manner. The Lhasa Apso can also be a watchdog.

Living conditions

Its quiet manner and small size make this Asian animal an ideal dog for a flat.

But this is more than just a lap dog and needs to exercise. It is known to get along well with children and with other dogs.

Pug

Size and build

A Pug can be about 30 cm (12 in) tall and weigh up to 7 or 8 kg (16–17.5 lb). The breed originated in China but has been a favourite with British royalty, among others, for centuries.

This well-known and much-loved companion dog is sturdy, strong and has a rather square shape. The Pug is muscular and has a broad back. The limbs are comparatively short.

The head is round and relatively large in relation to the body. The muzzle is very short, giving it its distinctive flat and wrinkled face.

Like other breeds with a stubby muzzle—such as the Pekingese and the Bulldog—the Pug may occasionally have difficulty swallowing and breathing.

Coat

The short, dense coat is quite soft. Favoured colours are silver-grey, apricot and a white-yellow, amongst others. Markings may be present, as well. The black mask is typical for the breed.

Character and disposition

The Pug has become a popular companion because of a host of agreeable traits. They are known to be sensitive, clever and lively. Moreover, they are highly loyal and playful.

Living conditions

A Pug can be easily kept in a flat. But it needs to be kept busy, of course, and should not go without exercise. It is known to be friendly toward children and

relatively uncomplicated when dealing with his own kind.

Papillon

Size and build

Although these toy spaniels are exquisitely small—they reach a height of about 20 cm (8 in) and weigh between 1.5 and 5 kg (3–11 lb)—their body is not delicate, but rather robust, with a well-balanced physique overall. The head has a short muzzle that tapers to a pointed end. A Papillon should not look leggy.

Coat

The Papillon has a robust coat of medium length. The hair is glossy and wavy, with a ruff of longer hair around the neck and tail. On the rest of its body the hair is of medium length. The typical coat colouration is white with markings in any other colour. A head that is predominantly white is considered a flaw.

Character and disposition

This small dog is brimful of joy and energy. It is very playful and can be trained easily. But it is also very sensitive and will be upset by fighting and rude behaviour. The Papillon develops a very close relationship with its owners.

Living conditions

You can certainly keep a Papillon in a flat but you should be aware that this little bundle of energy needs more exercise than other mini dogs.

The Papillon loves nothing more than good company. It can develop a good relationship with children so long as they don't handle the dog too roughly. This applies for other breeds as well, of course. The Papillon has no trouble with other dogs.

Pekingese (Peking Palasthund)

Size and build

The Pekingese is a tiny dog at just 15 to 25 cm (6–10 in) and about 5 kg (11 lb). It has a short, blunt head. The back slopes down toward the rear, while its legs are short with flat paws.

Coat

The Pekingese has abundant long hair, particularly around the neck and tail.

All colours are permitted, though if the coat is a solid colour, a black mask on the face is preferred. Tricoloured dogs are common.

Character and disposition

This toy breed is as loyal as it is in need of affection. It is also smart and sensitive, and makes an alert watchdog.

Living conditions

The Pekingese can be perfectly content living in a flat. Naturally, it needs regular exercise but is not a dog that has a strong urge to run. This dog will happily share a home with children or even other dogs.

Shih Tzu

Size and build

With a maximum height of 27 cm (10 in), this Asian dog does not get very tall. It reaches a weight of about 8 kg (17 lb). It has a sturdy appearance with its somewhat long, strong trunk. The limbs are quite short and big-boned.

There is an undeniable resemblance between the Shih Tzu and the Lhasa Apso.

Coat

The abundance of hair on this dog is eye-catching. Shih Tzus have a short, dense undercoat, while the top coat is long, thick and straight without any curls. The hair is especially thick around

the tail. All sorts of coat colourings can appear. A white blaze and white tip of the tail are especially typical.

Character and disposition

The Shih Tzu is a lively and attentive dog that bonds closely with

its owner. It is also distinguished by its watchfulness.

Living conditions

This dog is well suited for a flat. It enjoys the company of children and other pets.

Yorkshire Terrier

Size and build

These dogs do not grow to be very tall. A Yorkshire Terrier is up to 20 cm (8 in) in height and weighs very little, only about 1.5 to 2 kg (3–4.5 lb).

The head of a Yorkshire Terrier has a delicate shape with a wide jaw. Its body has a compact, rectangular build. The short limbs of these terriers are straight and end in round paws. Its carriage conveys a noticeable air of importance.

Coat

This dog's silky, long, smooth hair is glossy and often lies with a parting down the back.

The typical coat colour for Yorkshire Terriers is a combination of steel-blue and tan. The tan coloured hair tends to be lighter toward the tips.

Character and disposition

This intelligent little terrier is extremely lively and sociable. It enjoys playing and is known for its friendly and devoted nature. Moreover, in spite of its size, the Yorkshire Terrier is courageous and watchful.

109

Living conditions

You can keep the Yorkshire Terrier very comfortably in a smallish flat, but it is important for this dog to have opportunity to romp about on a daily basis. This is much more than a lap dog—generally speaking, it is too lively to be limited to that role. Yorkshire Terriers are said to get on very well with children and other dogs; indeed, they require a lot of human attention in order to thrive.

Miniature Pinscher

Size and build

The Miniature Pinscher grows to a height of about 25 to 30 cm (10–12 in) and reaches a weight of about 3 to 4 kg (6.5–9 lb).

It has a slender head with a jaw that tapers toward the front. The ears are small and set high on the head. This dog has a rather square form with straight front legs and clearly angled hind legs.

Coat

A smooth, short coat that lies close to the body is typical for the Miniature Pinscher.

The coat is either solid reddish brown or bicoloured, for example black with red-brown markings.

Grooming

The short, smooth coat requires virtually no maintenance. However, it is a good idea to wipe the dog down with a damp cloth from time to time.

Character and disposition

Since the Miniature Pinscher is not a large dog it can be perfectly happy living in a flat. Naturally, it needs activity and opportunities to run and exercise. Demanding of attention, it makes a spirited and lively pet.

Living conditions

If you train this pinscher lovingly, it will be eager to learn and will become a very pleasant companion dog.

Utility Dogs

Akita Inu

Size and build

This Japanese member of the utility class stands 57 to 69 cm (22–27 in) tall and weighs from 30 to 45 kg (66–99 lb).

Coat

The top coat is coarse and short, the undercoat soft. Akitas may be any colour, and a dark face and head are typical. No more than a third of the coat may be white.

Character and disposition

The Akita, the Japanese national dog, is independent, but highly devoted to its people. Bred to hunt big game, including bears,

its natural tendency toward aggression has not been completely lost, especially toward other members of its own species. It makes a good watchdog.

Living conditions

Akitas will benefit from vigorous and firm training. They may be kept even in a small flat as long as you allow for enough exercise.

Alaskan Malamute

Size and build

The Alaskan Malamute was bred for strength rather than speed, and is one of the strongest of the Nordic dog breeds. They reach a height of 56 to 64 cm (22–25 in) and weigh around 35 kg (77 lb). They have all the physical characteristics necessary to perform the difficult work of sled dogs.

Coat

The Alaskan Malamute has a thick top coat of medium length which is especially heavy around the neck and shoulders. White, black and wolf-grey are their colours.

Character and disposition

A devoted, obedient and loyal animal, the Alaskan Malamute is known to have occasional problems in relation to other dogs—

Chow Chow

Size and build

This well known Chinese dog stands just over 50 cm (20 in) on average and reaches a weight of 25 to 30 kg (55–66 lb). It has a powerful, rather stout body with well proportioned limbs that end in small round paws. The head is fairly wide with a medium-sized muzzle.

Coat

The Chow Chow has a very thick, soft coat. It has a mane around its neck and a bushy, curled tail. Dogs of this breed have solid-coloured coats of any of a wide range of colours.

They may have lighter hair on the lower part of their tail and on the backs of their legs.

Character and disposition

The Chow Chow is an independent dog that seeks out a close relationship only with its master and is often referred to as a one-person-dog. It prized its freedom highly and does not like to be subordinate or to be forced to do anything (though it can be persuaded). In other respects, the Chow Chow is a very calm, but vigilant breed.

especially those of the same sex. In contrast, however, this dog is playful when invited, and therefore gets along well with children.

Living conditions

The Alaskan Malamute can be seen as a rugged kind of companion. It feels most comfortable in a natural, non-urban environment. As is true of many other large dogs, it can get along in less then spacious living situations, but only if it is able to exercise to its hearts' content. It is important for this dog to experience a stable hierarchy within the family.

Living conditions

A dog of this breed feels quite comfortable in a generous-sized flat, though lots of activity and movement are necessary.

Although a Chow Chow does not always get along with other dogs, it may develop a fairly good relationship with children over time.

Eurasian

Size and build

This relatively recent dog breed stands 50 to 60 cm (20–24 in) tall at a weight of about 30 kg (66 lb). Its overall appearance is reminiscent of a rugged sled dog.

Coat

This dog's top coat is of medium length, while the undercoat is thick.

They come in a range of colours from red to fallow, wolf-grey, black and black with markings, especially above the eyes.

Character and disposition

The Eurasian is by far not as wild as it looks; in fact, it was purposefully bred in the 1960s in order to be a beautiful family dog and is a successful combination of its Chow Chow and spitz ancestors. The breed is sensitive, attentive and watchful, and thrives on human attention.

Living conditions

A Eurasian does well in a flat, assuming that enough exercise is provided. This is a good family dog because, in contrast to some of its ancestors, it is not a "one-man-dog". It gets along very well with children and other dogs.

Finnish Spitz

Size and build

This breed, extraordinarily popular in its native Finland, where it was bred centuries ago for hunting, can get as tall as 50 cm (20 in) and weighs about 15 kg (33 lb). Its build is solid but not heavy. The head is not large in comparison to the body, and the muzzle is pointed.

Coat

Fox red, chestnut red and golden red are typical colours for this breed. Certain white markings and black roan are allowed. The undercoat is thick and lies close to the skin, while the top coat stands out from the body.

115

Character and disposition

The Finnish Spitz is anything but quiet. On the contrary, it barks loudly and enthusiastically. This was an essential trait when it was out hunting, as it was bred to do. The Finnish Spitz is a robust, intelligent and watchful dog that

Greenland Dog (Eskimo Dog)

Size and build

These Nordic dogs can reach a height of about 60 cm (24 in) and may weigh 30 kg (66 lb) and more.

greatly enjoys human companionship and being part of a family.

Living conditions

The Finnish Spitz likes children, and in general there should be no trouble with other dogs. It does need a garden, or better still, farmland to run in.

The muscular body of the Greenland Dog looks powerful, but not at all heavy.

It has a wide head with strong jaws. The neck is quite strong as well, but not very long. The back is long and the slopes slightly toward the rump.

117

Coat

Greenland Dogs have thick hair with a tough straight top coat. The undercoat, by contrast, is soft. The colour variations for this breed are almost unlimited.

Character and disposition

A Greenland Dog can be considered an independent, rugged type and it can withstand many things. Its disposition is friendly, spontaneous and not at all opposed to hunting.

Living conditions

Bred to pull sleds in Arctic conditions, the Greenland Dog is not well adapted to be kept purely as a companion dog. All things considered, the Greenland is a classic working dog that is very loyal to its master. It needs an extraordinary amount of exercise and a task that corresponds with its natural instincts.

It does not always have a good relationship with other animals and may be somewhat unpredictable around them.

Karelian Bear Dog

Size and build

The Karelian Bear Dog, originally from Finland, grows no more than 60 cm (24 in) tall and can weigh up to 25 to 28 kg (55–62 lb). It has a very powerful trunk, a muscular, arched neck of medium length and a slightly elongated head with a muzzle that tapers off to a rather pointed nose. The limbs of this hunting dog are not very long in relation to the length of its body.

Coat

These Nordic dogs have a straight, stiff top coat. The undercoat, however, is soft and thick.

Some of the hair of the top coat is longer in several places: around the neck and on the throat and chest, at the back of the upper legs, as well as on the back and tail. The typical colouring is black with white markings including a blaze on the face. The Karelian Bear Dog has pointed teeth.

Character and disposition

Impetuous vivaciousness is a character trait of this dog, which is anything but shy and does not put up with any nonsense. The Karelian Bear Dog is an enthusiastic hunter as well. But all these qualities do not prevent it from developing obedience with consistent training. It is very loyal and affectionate toward its master.

Living conditions

This dog is not made for the life of an urban pet. It needs plentiful exercise and a task to perform. It can be trained to be a watchdog, for example, drawing on its courageous nature. It will defend house and property especially well.

Norwegian Buhund

Size and build

This dog is about 45 cm (18 in) tall and reaches a weight of about

20 kg (44 lb). Its build is agile and light without being over delicate. It has straight legs and its back, which is also straight, is of moderate length. The form of its head

119

clearly indicates that the Norwegian Buhund belongs to the group of Nordic spitz dogs.

Coat

The top coat of the Norwegian Buhund is rough and of medium length. It is preferable for it to be a single colour, but there may be some markings. Typical colours for this dog's coat are wheat, pale red and black.

Character and disposition

These herding dogs hardly seem to know what fear is. They are extremely courageous and vigilant and often develop great devotion. Their hunting instincts remain quite strong.

Living conditions

A lot of opportunity to move and a lot of space are very important for the Norwegian Buhund. It is well-suited to be a family dog as it can develop wonderful relationships with children. It may, however, not always be willing to get along well with other dogs.

Samoyed

Size and build

This Nordic dog, once bred to herd reindeer in northern Russia, can grow up to 56 cm (22 in) tall

and weigh about 20 to 30 kg (44–66 lb). The Samoyed has a powerful physique with straight limbs and a relatively large head.

Coat

White, cream as well as beige are typical Samoyed colourings. The top coat is full, straight, and quite hard compared to the soft, short undercoat.

Character and disposition

Vivaciousness and a friendly, devoted disposition distinguish the Samoyed. It often displays great stamina and an eagerness to work.

Living conditions

This dog is traditionally a herder and sled dog. If you keep it as a companion dog you will have to make sure this animal gets a lot of exercise. The Samoyed is friendly toward children and should be quite suitable as a family dog.

Schipperke

Size and build

A fully-grown Schipperke stands around 30 cm (12 in) tall and weighs up to just 8 kg (17.6 lb).

This dog has a very stocky trunk and a broad straight back. The croup is rounded and flows into a stubbed tail. The head of the Schipperke is similar to the head of a fox. Its paws are quite small but they are equipped with strong nails.

In addition to the standard Schipperke, there is also a somewhat smaller type that attains a shoulder height of about 24 cm (10 in).

Coat

The Shipperke should be pitch black; it is not bred in any other colour. The coat is dense, rough and short.

Long or silky hair is regarded as a breeding flaw. The coat can be

thicker around the neck than elsewhere on the body.

The Shipperke is a sturdy dog that does not require much special care, but an occasional brushing enhances the good condition of the coat.

Character and disposition

The Shipperke has a need to be involved in anything that goes on around it. It is curious, barks quite a bit and is very lively. This dog is highly devoted toward its people. But this is also a watchful dog and can be suspicious of strangers. The Shipperke is a courageous hunter of rats, mice, wild rabbits and more and doesn't hesitate to attack perceived enemies.

Living conditions

The Shipperke is very popular in its native country of Belgium, where it used to hunt rats and guard boats. It is comfortable as part of a family because it likes children. This dog can be kept in a city if you provide enough opportunity for exercise.

Siberian Husky

Size and build

These Nordic dogs reach a height of about 60 cm (24 in) and weigh between 15 and 25 kg (33–55 lb). Their body has a slight rectangular format with a moderately long neck and a medium-sized head. Their limbs are solid and end in relatively large paws.

Coat

The straight top coat is soft and fine. White, black and all shades in between as well as a sandy colour can occur, with markings of all sorts.

Grooming

Brushing and combing the coat occasionally keeps it in a well-groomed condition.

Character and disposition

The Siberian Husky is an even-tempered dog that enjoys human companionship. Bred to pull sledges on the tundra, it is a tireless worker with an extremely high energy level. It retains a certain independence, even stubbornness, but with patience can be trained.

Living conditions

If a Siberian Husky as a working dog, you will have to provide it with other kinds of activity and exercise. This dog is known to be adaptable and unproblematic when dealing with children.

Other Breeds

Dobermann (Doberman Pinscher)

Size and build

Animals of this breed generally get to be between 60 and 70 cm (24–28 in) tall and they can reach a weight of up to 45 kg (100 lb). The Dobermann has a deep chest and a short, firm back section with a rounded rump.

The front legs are quite straight, but the back legs have angulated hocks. Overall, a Dobermann makes a powerful impression, neither massive nor light.

Coat

The coat of a Dobermann is not supposed to be soft; instead it is smooth, hard, thick and short-haired. Dobermanns may be black, brown or blue with brown or tan markings.

Character and disposition

Bred as the ultimate guard dog, nervousness and suspicion of strangers may be elements of a Dobermann's personality, but they are reliably and intensely loyal toward their owners. This breed is also distinguished by its liveliness, courage and stamina, as well as its quick comprehension.

Living conditions

Not surprisingly, a small flat is not the right place to keep a Dobermann. It needs space to move and a house with a garden is a more appropriate place for it. The Dobermann is especially well-suited for training as a protective dog or watchdog and will respond to careful training for these roles. If the dog is not used for these tasks, it will still need good, firm training—which does not mean unnecessary harshness, but specialised knowledge of how

to deal with these dogs. For all their power, they are usually quite good with children.

Kromfohrlaender

Size and build

This German dog reaches a height of up to 46 cm (18 in). It has a well-proportioned build with a straight, strong back. The muzzle tapers slightly toward the front, but does not look pointed. The legs are slender in comparison to the body.

Coat

A short, wirehaired coat is typical of the Kromfohrlaender, though there is also a less popular straighthaired type with longer fur. The hair is a bit longer on the chest and muzzle of the wirehaired form. The standard colouration is white with patches in various shades of tan on the head and on the back.

Character and disposition

The Kromfohrlaender has a host of traits that make it a wonderful companion. It is a highly energetic, active and attentive dog that has a well-balanced disposition. It is intelligent, an excellent watchdog, and will defend its surroundings.

Living conditions

Sufficient movement and a purposeful activity work magic for this dog, as for so many other terriers. If you can provide your dog with these things then you can keep the Kromfohrlaender in a flat. It may have a tendency to become more attached to one person above all others, but is still well-suited to be a family dog.

Poodle

Size and build

There are three types of the well known and popular Poodle: Standard Poodles are the largest, getting taller than 60 cm (24 in). Miniature Poodles are smaller than that, and Toy Poodles are very small, less than 30 cm (12 in) high. Their weight, of course, varies with their size and lies

125

between 4 and 30 kg (9–66 lb). The body of the Poodle seems rather square, on the whole. The neck is not extremely long and the back is rather short. Its limbs are strong and muscular. They end in oval paws.

Coat

The coat of the Poodle is long, luxurious and requires more care than most. It has a woolly feel to it and on clipped dogs will have curls. Traditional coat colours for this breed are black, white, silver, chestnut brown and apricot.

Character and disposition

The Poodle is a spirited and energetic dog with keen intelligence and a grand capacity to learn. Moreover, it will often become unusually devoted.

Living conditions

The Poodle has been transformed from a utility dog into the classic companion and family dog. According to its size, it is more or less amenable to life in a flat.

Schnauzers

Size and build

Schnauzers come in three sizes: Giant, Standard (from which the others are derived) and Miniature. Their height ranges from 30 to 70 cm (12–28 in); Standards are around 48 cm (19 in). Weight varies with their size, and can be anywhere from 5 to 35 kg (11–77 lb). All the Schnauzers have many traits in common.

Coat

The coat of a Schnauzer is wiry and protects the dog from various weather conditions. The hair is of medium length and not too close to its body, but longer on the face and legs. Typical colours for its coat are black and salt and pepper.

Character and disposition

Although Schnauzers were originally bred as working dogs, they are also a watchful breed, tending to be bold and proud. They are also playful and good natured.

on them in thick, loose folds. Animal advocates regard this extremely loose skin as problematic. They object that some of the folds over the eyes of Shar Pei puppies have to be sown up or even surgically removed.

Coat

The hair of the Shar Pei is short and comparatively hard. The coat is typically sandy coloured, deer brown, dark brown or even black.

Living conditions

Over time, Schnauzers have become popular family dogs. They enjoy an environment that includes many children. Not only the Giant Schnauzer, but the smaller ones as well, are very lively and need a lot of exercise. Without ample opportunity to run and exercise none of the Schnauzers will be happy.

Shar Pei

Size and build

This dog grows to a height of 40 to 50 cm (16–20 in), weighing between 15 and 20 kg (33–44 lb). It has a rectangular shape with limbs that are not too short. Very typical—and in this extreme form only existent in this particular breed—is their skin, which hangs

Character and disposition

Shar Pei are known to be fine creatures with pleasant traits. They are gentle, loyal and loving. They need a lot of love and firm training. Generally calm, they can also be very playful.

Suitable surroundings

Its great love for children makes the Shar Pei a wonderful family dog. If possible it should be kept in a house with a garden.

Index